TFILE

NEWCASTLE

PACKED WITH INFORMATION ON THE MAGPIES

FACTFILE
NEWCASTLE

This edition published and distributed by Parragon, 1998

Parragon
Unit 13-17 Avonbridge Trading Estate
Atlantic Road
Avonmouth
Bristol BS11 9QD

Produced by Magpie Books,
an imprint of Robinson Publishing Ltd, London

ISBN 0 75252 552 2

A copy of the British Library Cataloguing-in-Publication Data is available from the British Library.

Printed and bound in the EC.

This independent publication has been prepared without any involvement on the part of Newcastle United Football Club or the FA Premier League.

FACTFILE

NEWCASTLE

PACKED WITH INFORMATION ON THE MAGPIES

Peter Gamble

PARRAGON

CONTENTS

Introduction

Look at the history books and you'd be forgiven for thinking Newcastle United are a sleeping giant. They haven't topped the pile at the end of the season since the 1920s, while silverware of any description has been a rare sight in the St James' Park boardroom in recent years.

But winning isn't everything, and the entertainment provided by the Magpies over the last century and a bit has been breathtaking, players from Hughie Gallagher through Milburn to Keegan, Waddle and Gascoigne and, of course, £15 million man Alan Shearer.

Player turned manager Kevin Keegan brought the England Number 9 to St James', along with the most success the club had seen in decades – and it's currently down to Kenny Dalglish to keep that going. This book dips back into the Keegan era and beyond, highlighting the triumphs and tragedies, successes and failures and the players and managers who made the headlines...all divided into easily digestible sections to entertain as well as inform.

As the mighty Magpies look to add honours to their reputation for entertainment, this book gives a flavour of their pulsating past.

Goals Galore!

Though they've been under-achievers in silverware terms over the years, Newcastle United have always been known as an attacking outfit whose players know the way to goal.

When Andy Cole racked up his 40th goal of 1993-94 to break George Robledo's and Hughie Gallagher's long-standing club record of 39 goals in a season, he confirmed his status in Geordie folklore. Cole's stay at the club was relatively brief and he found goals more difficult to come by after leaving, but his Magpies total of 55 in 70 League appearances compares favourably with any of the club greats.

Hughie Gallagher's goalscoring feats for United still stand as the club's most impressive, for in the five seasons from 1925-26 to 1929-30 he scored a total of 143 goals in 174 League and Cup games. His second season yielded a club record 39 achieved in 41 games, including four hat-tricks and one four-goal haul. Albert Stubbins' figures of 237 goals in 218 appearances may appear to be the greater achievement, but most of his successes came during the Second World War when the opposition was not always of the highest quality. That said, his tally of over 40 goals in four successive seasons is still a statistic which should not be overlooked.

George Robledo's record-equalling haul of 1951-52 comprised 33 goals in 39 League games and six in seven Cup ties, including the winning goal in the Final against Arsenal. In one purple patch in September, United scored 19 times in four League games with Robledo snatching 11 goals. His total of 91 goals in 164 appearances would make him the envy of most strikers today.

In the all-time scorers list Jackie Milburn remains at the top of the tree with 238 in nearly 500 appearances, including wartime football. Although he never topped 28 goals in any one season, his consistency over his 14-year spell at St James' Park was undeniable. Milburn was the season's leading scorer on five occasions, an achievement matched by Hughie Gallagher and Len White.

'Wor Jackie' scored on his debut for England in 1949 and a year later bagged a hat-trick against Wales. In the same two seasons he played for the Football League against the Irish League, scoring three times in both games. He is also credited with one of the fastest ever strike for the Magpies, hitting the net in just ten seconds versus Cardiff City in a Division Two game in 1947. He also registered one of the club's best individual scoring records with six goals in a friendly against Alberta during a tour of Canada.

Len White, a Gallowgate favourite through the 1950s into the early 1960s, packed 120 of his goals into the five seasons when he was leading scorer. He stands second only to Jackie Milburn in the all-time League and Cup rankings, and while he shares with him the fact that he never scored 30 goals in any one season, he scored a hat-trick on the opening day of the 1960-61 campaign. He's also one of the few Newcastle players to have scored a first-half hat-trick, while three more goals came his way within eight minutes in 1958 as he starred for the Football League against the Irish League.

The 121 goals Malcolm Macdonald scored for United puts him at number four in the table of top scorers. 'Supermac' is credited with probably the fastest goal on record, netting with a shot from the centre circle in a friendly against St Johnstone with only four seconds on the watch. In the 1974-75 campaign, he recorded his best season's total for United with 27, and that April planted himself firmly in the record books with five goals for England versus Cyprus. He kicked off the following season in fine style too, the first four games bringing him six goals.

Many United players have impressive strike rates, including Vic Keeble, Kevin Keegan and Mick Quinn, all of whom averaged a goal every other game. Quinn topped the Football League chart in season 1989-90, notching up 34 goals in 53 games. In the 1920s, centre-forward Neil Harris became the scourge of opposition defences with over 100 goals to his credit, while in the following decade Jack Smith became the toast of St James' Park, scoring 73 times in only 112 outings. Len Shackleton had a brief but telling stay with United, his debut bringing him six goals including a 155-second hat-trick against Newport in 1946, still the fastest in first-class football. Until his serious injury problems Alan Shearer looked ready to re-write the record books, as 27 goals came his way in 1996-97.

Looking further back into Magpies history, Albert Shepherd, an England international, scored 92 goals in only 123 games before the First World War and would probably have had many more but for a serious injury that kept him out of the game for a considerable period. He was following in the goalscoring footsteps of Bill Appleyard, who netted 87 times in 145 appearances.

United have recorded double figures in a game on a number of occasions, notably 16 in the Alberta game where Milburn bagged six. Only once has this been achieved in the League – a 13-0 scoreline against Newport County in 1946 which seems unlikely to be beaten against today's well-drilled defences. That season United scored a total of 109 goals in League and Cup, yet when they bettered it in 1951-52 with 113, they surprisingly finished only eighth in Division One. The FA Cup was some consolation.

Through The Years
January

1909
January

During their third Championship season, United won all six League and Cup fixtures played in January, scoring 18 times with only one goal conceded.

1934
January
1

This New Year's Day fixture saw the amazing scoreline of Newcastle 9 Liverpool 2, after the teams had gone in level at half-time. Both Jimmy Richardson and Sammy Weaver helped themselves to hat-tricks. This result did nothing towards helping United avoid relegation.

1956
January
28

A thrilling FA Cup tie against Fulham at Craven Cottage ended 5-4 to Newcastle. The following year would bring another epic Cup-tie, this time against the holders, ending in another 5-4 win. Manchester City were beaten in this Maine

Road replay after extra-time, having led by three goals after 30 minutes.

1959
January
31

Len White scored twice as the Magpies rescued a 4-1 half-time deficit to draw 4-4 at Old Trafford. The same month of the following year would see White bag a hat-trick in a 7-3 drubbing of Manchester United before 57,200 fans at St James' Park.

1973
January

Terry McDermott signed for his first stint on Tyneside. He arrived from Bury for the bargain fee of £25,000.

1976
January

United played a total of nine League and Cup fixtures in the month, losing only one, to Tottenham in the first leg of the League Cup Semi-Final. Alan Gowling scored nine goals and the club was watched by a total of 323,239 fans.

DREAM TEAM 1

This United line-up of the early 1950s could hardly fail to be included in anyone's list of great teams, having just the right combination of talent and steely resolve. The secret of their FA Cup win and fourth place in Division One revolved around a settled side.

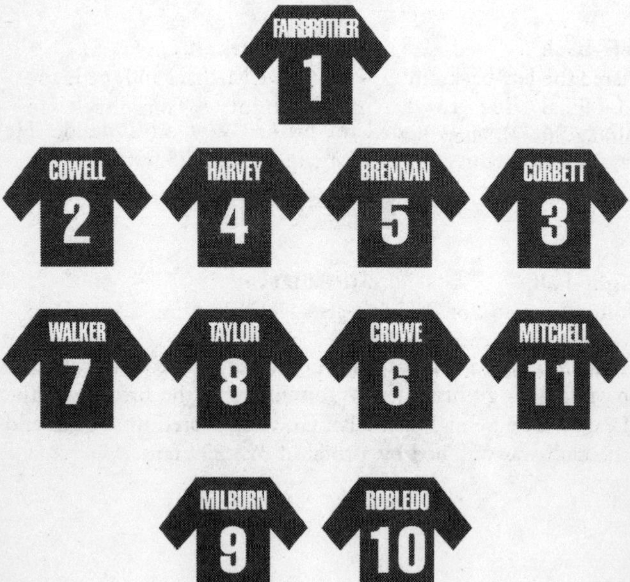

Goalkeeper **Jack Fairbrother**

A high-class keeper who was also part of the team which won promotion in 1947-48. Moved to Peterborough in 1952, being replaced by Ronnie Simpson.

Right-back **Bobby Cowell**

Played over 400 games for United and became a three-time Cup winner. Injured during the 1955 close-season and forced to retire.

Left-back **Bobby Corbett**

Shared the left-back duties with Alf McMichael and made the '51 Final due to his rival's injury. Transferred to Middlesbrough later that year.

Right-half **Joe Harvey**

United captain for eight years, Harvey inspired all those around him during some of the club's most exciting times. Destined to become player-coach in 1953 and nine years later team manager.

Centre-half **Frank Brennan**
Not a lot got past Scottish international Frank Brennan, for whom the word 'stopper' was probably devised.

Left-half **Charlie Crowe**
A player who spent a dozen seasons at St James' Park, whose appearances were often hampered by injury. He still played in over 200 matches.

Outside-right **Tommy Walker**
A performer with great pace, Walker also made over 200 appearances, scoring 40 goals in the process.

Inside-right **Ernie Taylor**
A small but highly-skilled player, Taylor's greatest asset was his weight of pass. Went on to play for Blackpool and Manchester United, with whom he tasted Wembley victory and defeat in turn.

Centre-forward **Jackie Milburn**
A legendary figure who won so many plaudits in his day, all totally deserved. A credit to United and the game in general.

Inside-left **George Robledo**

Although often wearing the Number 10 shirt, Robledo was almost like a secondary centre-forward, snatching goals on a regular basis in lethal combination with Milburn. Scored the winning goal in the 1952 Cup Final.

Outside-left **Bobby Mitchell**

Carries legendary status on Tyneside alongside Milburn. The crowd loved his weaving runs and appreciated every one of his 113 goals scored in 13 seasons.

APPEARANCES

The Bosman ruling and fat signing-on fees make loyalty a rare commodity in today's game. Yet history has shown that, with a support as loyal as the Magpies', players who dedicate their career to the club are assured of appreciation.

Goalkeeper Jimmy Lawrence, capped once by Scotland, heads the all-time list of appearances for the club with a total of 505, consisting of 432 in the League, 64 Cup games and nine in wartime football. He also holds the record for consecutive FA Cup ties with 46 and played in five Finals, only managing one winner's medal. His presence enabled United to win the Division One trophy in 1906-07, while he was ever-present in League and Cup in three separate seasons. Lawrence had already performed for three Scots clubs before arriving at St James' Park.

Not far behind in Magpie colours comes full-back Frank Hudspeth, with 482 appearances between 1910 and 1928. He played in the same line-up as Lawrence for a number of seasons and became club captain in 1923. He won both League and Cup winner's medals, being capped by England at the age of 35. He also managed to score 38 goals in his Newcastle career, eight in one season – not bad for a defender.

In the modern era, full-back Frank Clark sits on top of the tree, although he had 23 European games to boost his total to 457. He was part of the successful Magpie team that won the Second Division title in 1964-65, being ever-present at left-back, and appeared in all 12 games as United lifted the Inter-Cities Fairs Cup four seasons later. After leaving Newcastle, he won further honours with Nottingham Forest, whom he later managed.

Full-backs seem to figure strongly where United appearance records are concerned, for Billy McCracken also played over 400 games during the Lawrence/Hudspeth era. Irish international McCracken shares a record with fellow full-back Billy Hampson, as when they took the field against Cardiff City on 10 February 1923, they became the oldest full-back partnership in Football League history, both being 40 years of age. (Perhaps the fact that United lost 5-0 could be significant.)

Hampson also has the distinction of being the oldest player ever to appear for the Magpies, being 44 years and 220 days old when facing Birmingham on 9 April 1927. His other claims to fame include being the oldest scorer for United, against Middlesbrough aged 41 in 1923, while the following year saw him become the oldest Cup-winning medallist at 41 years and eight months. With the demands of the modern game, both of these records should stand forever.

Returning to the modern era, right-back David Craig played for no other League club, making his debut against Cardiff City in November 1963 and playing his final game for the black and whites 14 years later versus Arsenal. His 412 appearances plus 25 internationals for Northern Ireland would almost certainly have been bettered but for injury.

The only other two 400-plus men are Alf McMichael and Bobby Mitchell. Mitchell claimed three FA Cup winner's medals and McMichael one as they made major contributions to the Magpies' cause throughout the 1950s and into the 1960s.

On four occasions Mitchell appeared in 40 or more games in a season, 50 in 1954-55. When he left Newcastle in 1963 McMichael was the most capped player in the club's history, having played 40 times for Northern Ireland.

What about Jackie Milburn you might say? Yes, Jackie did appear in nearly 500 games for United but only 397 were in League and Cup: approximately 100 took place during the war years and are therefore not part of official records.

Heading the list of consecutive appearances is midfielder Tommy Gibb who signed up for the 1968-69 season, missing the very first League game but then completing 171 games in succession. The closest anyone has come to this record is

Bryan Robson, who coincidentally started his run of 148 a little earlier in 1968. After these two come Alan Kennedy and Chris Waddle with 121 and 106 respectively.

A player who may have aspired to enter the St James' Park record books was Paul Ferris, the club's youngest ever debutant when he came on as a substitute against Blackburn on 1 May 1982 at the tender age of 16 years 295 days. Alas he left the club in September 1986, having made the starting line-up once, served as a substitute in 12 games and scored one goal.

Others who made their debuts before their 18th birthday were Alan Suddick, Jock Rutherford and Neil McDonald, all of whom distinguished themselves for the club. Colin Clish was just 17 when he made the first team but departed after only 23 games.

The oldest player ever to debut for United was Andy Cunningham, acquired from Rangers and 38 years and three days old when appearing against Leicester on 2 February 1929. He retired 15 games and two goals later.

At the start of the 1997-98 season, long-serving Rob Lee was fast approaching the 200 League game mark for the Magpies, having notched nearly 300 more with Charlton. Would he be there for the millennium? Only time will tell...

Through The Years
February

1905
February

The first year United made the FA Cup Final saw them take a roundabout road to Crystal Palace, then the Final venue. In the space of 19 days in February they played five Cup ties, eventually overcoming Plymouth Argyle in three attempts and Tottenham in two. They also managed a League game in that period as well!

1932
February
1

United scored seven goals in 25 minutes in an FA Cup Fourth Round second replay against Southport at Hillsborough, Jimmy Richardson notching a hat-trick in the 9-0 rout. The previous two games had finished level at 1-1. A further eight goals were scored in the other two ties that month, indicating the Magpies were making a serious Cup bid.

1951
February

Goalkeeper Ronnie Simpson signed from Third Lanark to start a spell of close on ten years at St James' Park. Simpson had played for Queen's Park at the tender age of 14 and was destined to enter the record books again when, at the age of 36, he became Scotland's oldest international. He played in a total of nearly 300 games for United and collected two Cup winner's medals.

1952
February

Vic Keeble joined United from Colchester for a fee of £15,000. Keeble was a fearless, combative old-style centre-forward who scored 67 goals in 120 appearances before moving to West Ham. He bagged a Cup winner's medal in 1955 and headed the club goalscoring table in 1955-56.

1997
February
2

Alan Shearer had already served notice that his predatory powers had not waned since his move to United in 1996 – and, in the last 14 minutes of the Leicester game, underlined the fact by scoring a hat-trick.

Great Strikers

There's nothing the St James' Park faithful love better than a prolific goalscorer – and over the years they've had more than their fair share. Let's take a look at the most notable Number 9s.

Bill Appleyard

Appleyard came from the days when strikers were known simply as forwards and the leader of the attack generally fitted the same mould whichever club you turned to – over six foot tall and around the 14 stone mark

Appleyard typified the fearless centre-forward of the day; perhaps the best comparison would be likening him to a less sophisticated version of Malcolm Macdonald. His speciality seems to have been taking on the goalkeeper with physical challenges of the kind now outlawed in the game.

In 1903, the ex-fisherman joined United from Grimsby Town and was immediately introduced into a side regarded as the best of its era. The goals did not take long to start to flow, 16 in 31 League games in 1903-04 and 15 in League and Cup in the following Championship season. His ratio per game rose even higher as United's dominance secured another title but he failed to win an FA Cup winners' medal, having to make do with second best in 1905 and missing the 1906 showcase, when his goals were one of the reasons United had made it to the Final. In 1908, he scored eight goals in five rounds up to the Final but failed to find the mark on another occasion where the Magpies failed to do themselves justice.

In the summer of 1908, still regarded as a force to be reckoned with, Bill Appleyard left for Oldham. His departure affected United not at all, as they recorded yet another Championship win less than 12 months later. He returned to the north-east to work in the Vickers factory and died perhaps fittingly, in Newcastle towards the end of the 1950s.

BILL APPLEYARD UNITED RECORD 1903-08									
League		FA Cup		League Cup		Europe		Total	
Apps	Goals	Apps	Goals	Apps	Goals	Apps	Goals	Apps	Goals
128	71	17	16	—	—	—	—	145	87

Jackie Milburn

Jackie was perhaps the most famous member of the Milburn dynasty that so dominated English football in the 1950s; this included his cousins George, who made League appearances for Chesterfield, James, who played for Leeds United and Bradford Park Avenue, and John, who played for Norwich and Bradford City (all three were brothers), as well as the two Charlton brothers, Jackie and Bobby.

Born John ET Milburn in 1924 in Ashington, a town which had produced famous footballers out of all proportion to its size, he joined Newcastle United straight from school but lost a good few years as the Second World War cut into his career. He finally made his League debut when the competition resumed in 1946-47, initially alongside Charlie Wayman, who would lead the Second Division goalscorers list with 30 goals. Wayman's sudden departure after he had been dropped for the 1947 Semi-Final against Charlton (which

United lost 4–0) thrust Milburn into the spotlight, and he clearly relished the prospect.

Newcastle returned to the top flight as Second Division runners-up in 1947–48, consolidated their position over the next two seasons and then embarked on what was seemingly an endless Cup-tie for the next half decade. They won the FA Cup in 1951, depriving Blackpool 2–0, with Jackie (as he was known throughout his career to differentiate him from his cousin John) scoring both goals.

They then became the first club this century to retain the Cup, beating Arsenal 1–0 the following season, with Chilean George Robledo scoring the only goal. In 1955, Jackie, along with Bob Cowell and Bobby Mitchell, picked up his third Cup winner's medal in five seasons, scoring United's first in the 3–1 win over Manchester City.

In 1956 Milburn brought his Newcastle career to a close, having made 353 League appearances and scored 177 goals. He had made his England debut in 1948–49 and went on to win 13 caps, scoring ten goals. More than anything, Jackie Milburn, or 'Wor Jackie' as he was known on Tyneside, helped define the role of the centre-forward at Newcastle. Unknowingly, he created high expectations which many a Newcastle striker has had to contend with ever since: fans had to wait until Malcolm Macdonald for someone able to fill his boots.

Jackie Milburn certainly lived up to his initials (JET) with a blistering turn of pace. He was also an exceptional header of the ball, often able to rise head and shoulders above defenders and beat the goalkeeper. Newcastle's finest postwar centre-forward passed away in 1988.

JACKIE MILBURN UNITED RECORD 1946–57

League		FA Cup		League Cup		Europe		Total	
Apps	Goals	Apps	Goals	Apps	Goals	Apps	Goals	Apps	Goals
353	177	44	23	—	—	—	—	397	200

Bobby Mitchell

If their is one thing Geordie football fans enjoy, it is the sight of the talented individual unveiling his bag of tricks simply for the public's pleasure – and in Bobby Mitchell they had a player who very rarely failed to entertain. In fact, the main reason why Mitchell took to the game in the first place revolved around his belief that football was, first and foremost, something to be enjoyed. No player with his on-pitch persona could have approached the game otherwise.

Given his ability, he just had to take players on and invariably he would leave defenders in his wake as he bore down on goal or put in the telling cross.

United paid Third Lanark £16,000 in 1949 for his services, and Mitchell's contribution to the three successful FA Cup runs of the 1950s was invaluable. The 3-1 win over Manchester City in 1955 saw him score the all-important second goal. Like Willie McFaul, he had the misfortune to vie for an international place with a legend in his own lifetime, in his case Billy Liddell, so chances were limited. However, in 1951 he made two appearances, against France and Denmark – little reward for a player of his talents.

Mitchell played his last game for United in March 1961, when relegation loomed and his own speed of thought had started to deteriorate. He headed north to Berwick in the summer but returned to the north-east for a spell as player-manager with Gateshead. If Liddell became a legend on Merseyside, Mitchell fitted the bill perfectly for Tynesiders.

BOBBY MITCHELL UNITED RECORD 1949-61

League		FA Cup		League Cup		Europe		Total	
Apps	Goals	Apps	Goals	Apps	Goals	Apps	Goals	Apps	Goals
367	95	41	18	—	—	—	—	408	113

Bryan 'Pop' Robson

During the course of his career Bryan Robson became known as a goalpoacher supreme, both in his United period and after moving on to a series of other clubs. His debut season, 1964-65, could hardly have been more favourable: he scored in his first game, made 20 starts, grabbed seven goals and became part of a promotion-winning side.

United made heavy weather of those first couple of seasons back in the top flight, but opposing defences started to look at the Magpies' attack with renewed respect after Wyn Davies and Robson built up a rapport. The Fairs Cup win of 1968-69 owed much to their goals in the early rounds.

In his seven seasons, Robson finished top scorer on four occasions, his best haul coming in 1968-69 with 30 goals from 59 appearances: this was rivalled by the 25 netted in 52 games in 1969-70. He became one of the deadliest finishers in the game, likened to Jimmy Greaves in his heyday. Leaving in the middle of yet another of those conflicts involving player and management, he became a West Ham striker in the early part of 1971 and continued to bag goals regularly.

Robson had over 300 goals to his credit when he finally quit playing. He never gained full international honours, having to make do with a couple of Under-23 caps and a Football League representative appearance, so joining the long list of distinguished players who never made it into the ultimate arena. Maybe Robson was the unluckiest of all, given his track record at the highest domestic level.

BRYAN 'POP' ROBSON UNITED RECORD 1962-71

League		FA Cup		League Cup		Europe		Total	
Apps	Goals	Apps	Goals	Apps	Goals	Apps	Goals	Apps	Goals
206	82	10	4	4	2	24	9	244	97

ALAN SHEARER

When Kevin Keegan arrived at St James' Park as a player he was greeted as a saviour. How fitting, then, that he should be the manager who bought Alan Shearer, the player viewed as the final piece in the Magpies' jigsaw.

If people raised an eyebrow at the world record fee, Tyneside fans will look back with a satisfied smile if his goals do secure the big one. Keegan knew exactly what he was getting in the summer of 1996, for Shearer is a proven goalscorer at both club and international level, his 23 goals in 118 League games at Southampton having long been eclipsed by the 112 in 138 for Blackburn. His England record is equally impressive, with 16 strikes in 35 appearances.

His first season could not have been better as 27 goals came his way and Les Ferdinand benefited from his considerable presence. Their goals were not enough to win the elusive title, though, as the runners-up spot was again Newcastle's niche.

This striking axis was to last for only one season, however, as Ferdinand headed back to London and Shearer's injury kept him sitting on the sidelines. A player of Shearer's class would be missed by any club but, as United struggled through the winter months, the battle to get him fit became paramount – not least from England's World Cup point of view.

In January 1998 he could at last be seen back in a United shirt amid speculation regarding his level of fitness, but completed his first appearances without alarm. The hopes of club and country alike rested on his broad shoulders.

ALAN SHEARER UNITED RECORD 1996-(97)									
League		FA Cup		League Cup		Europe		Total	
Apps	Goals	Apps	Goals	Apps	Goals	Apps	Goals	Apps	Goals
31	25	3	1	1	1	3	—	38	27

BEST SEASON 1

In many respects, the third First Divison Championship of the early 1900s was the most remarkable, not least because United never dropped below third position and, after late January, were never headed.

The previous season had ended somewhat disappointingly with only three wins in the last 14 games, the Magpies' Championship challenge dying accordingly and a fourth-place finish being the consequence. So when the new season opened with five consecutive victories, it was obvious that United were throwing down the gauntlet to their rivals at a very early stage – and when the lethal Albert Shepherd was signed from Bolton the challenge clearly heightened. Shepherd was already an England player when arriving at St James' Park and, like Alan Shearer more recently, brought with him a reputation as a fearless, free-scoring centre-forward.

Scoring in his first game, a 4-0 away win over Nottingham Forest at the end of November, Shepherd looked like the man to ensure another successful season. He also scored in the next game, but unfortunately this was the 9-1 record reverse against rivals Sunderland which could well have unsettled lesser sides. Bearing in mind that United only conceded 41 goals in 38 games, the result was all the more remarkable. Instead of undermining the club's confidence, the defeat only acted as a spur: only one loss was sustained in the next 16 games, including a run of seven wins where only one goal was conceded.

Undoubtedly, Shepherd's contribution helped United to another victorious season. He scored 11 goals in 14 games, but the likes of Colin Veitch, scorer of nine goals wearing the Number 5 shirt, and the goalkeeping of Jimmy Lawrence played an important part. Only 65 goals were scored in total, fewer than five other sides, including Manchester City who finished second to bottom – proof of how important a good solid defence was, even in those less cautious days.

United eventually won the League title by seven points from Everton, with Sunderland third, and were even allowed the luxury of losing four out of their last six games. Clearly, that 16-game run had been the deciding factor in clinching the title in a season which could have been even more remarkable had Manchester United been overcome in the FA Cup Semi-Final.

1908-09 LEAGUE RECORD		
Opponents	**Home**	**Away**
Aston Villa	0-2	0-3
Blackburn Rovers	2-0	4-2
Bradford City	1-0	2-1
Bristol City	2-1	3-3
Bury	3-1	1-1
Chelsea	1-3	2-1
Everton	3-0	1-0
Leicester Fosse	2-0	4-0
Liverpool	0-1	1-2
Manchester City	2-0	2-0
Manchester United	2-1	0-1
Middlesbrough	1-0	0-0
Nottingham Forest	1-1	4-0
Notts County	1-0	4-0
Preston North End	2-0	1-0
Sheffield United	4-0	1-1
Sheffield Wednesday	1-0	0-2
Sunderland	1-9	1-3
Woolwich Arsenal	3-1	2-1

DERBY FOCUS

The Magpies' previous incarnation, East End, had played the majority of its games against local opposition, so it should come as no surprise that the newly titled Newcastle United Football Club played its first ever game versus Middlesbrough on 24 December 1892.

This friendly saw Newcastle post a 2-1 win – but one month later in the FA Cup against the same opposition, Boro ran out 3-2 victors. The 1893-94 season, the club's baptism in Division Two, saw local rivals Middlesbrough Ironopolis beaten 7-2 in January during a five-match winning run. Two seasons on, the qualifying rounds of the FA Cup saw United's pride be boosted by 8-0 and 4-1 victories over West Hartlepool NER and Middlesbrough respectively.

So local derbies were starting to become an established part of the football in the north-east, but it was not until United's inaugural season in Division One that Sunderland had to be faced. Christmas Eve 1898 proved an auspicious date, as the team destined to become United's most bitter rivals were overcome 3-2 at Roker Park, the goals being shared by Peddie (two) and Wardrope. As is often the way, Sunderland sneaked a win at St James' Park on the last day of the season with the only goal of the game.

During the first decade of the 20th century, United became one of the major footballing forces in the land but generally shared the spoils when confronted with their local rivals. The galling aspect of their first Championship-winning season in 1904-05 must have been losing to Sunderland twice, 3-1 in both games, though Middlesbrough proved no obstacle to their ambitions. United brought the title back to Tyneside two years later, but Sunderland were to inflict a memorable trouncing during the next Championship season of 1908-09.

A keenly fought local derby played on 5 December 1908 in front of 56,000 supporters was nicely poised at 1-1 as half-time arrived. Nobody in the ground suspected the goal avalanche they were about to witness until, in the space of 28 second-half minutes, Sunderland scored eight goals to run out 9-1 winners. Strangely this aberration had little effect on the title march, for 13 wins came the Magpies way in the next 15 League games. In terms of local pride, however, this defeat would take many years to avenge.

Losing derby games is a painful experience under any circumstances, but results tend to balance out over a period of years. The Christmas games of 1914, for instance, saw United face Sunderland twice, losing at home on Christmas Day by 5-2 and reversing the result by 4-2 on Boxing Day.

In the post-Gallagher season of 1930-31, Middlesbrough put eight goals past the Magpies and a rampant Sunderland at Roker Park demolished them 5-0. At the end of the 1933-34 series United were relegated, and it was not until after promotion was won in the 1948-49 season that League hostilities recommenced among the north-east elite.

The years of the Second World War had produced many local derbies due to regionalisation, clubs playing the same sides up to half-a-dozen times a season. The quality of the football may not have come from the top drawer, but which Magpie fan wouldn't have got a buzz from successive scorelines against Middlesbrough of 7-0 and 7-4, not to mention an 8-2 in 1944?

Christmas 1955 went a long way to erasing the memory of the 9-1 drubbing United had received at the hands of Sunderland in 1908. On Boxing Day, the Magpies inflicted a 6-1 beating at Roker Park, leading 3-0 within 18 minutes and generally bossing the game throughout, even though Bobby Mitchell carried an injury throughout the second half. Curry, Keeble and Milburn all scored twice in one of the club's most satisfying results to date.

Keeble and Milburn were on target again the following day as Sunderland capitulated 3-1. Unfortunately, the euphoria was slightly dampened the following March when the Wearsiders dumped United out of the Cup.

In the next couple of years the Tynesiders did not have the happiest of times in Division One, the only compensation for finishing 19th in 1957-58 being Sunderland's relegation. The Charlie Mitten era petered out and 1961-62 found the three major forces in the north-east doing battle in Division Two, the first time they had all been in the same division for a number of years. United celebrated by failing to win any of the four derby games.

Only three seasons were spent outside the top flight before United bounced back, a year after Sunderland had returned.

The threesome continued to cross each others' paths in subsequent years, United fans finding 1979-80 a painful experience as Sunderland won the Second Division title (United finished ninth after earlier topping the table) and inflicted League Cup replay defeat at St James' Park in a tie decided on penalties.

In his first derby match for United, Kevin Keegan lined up alongside Mick Channon in a home fixture against Middlesbrough in 1982, Channon scoring in a 1-1 draw. And who will forget the 1985 New Year's Day clash with Sunderland which brought Peter Beardsley a hat-trick in a match which had all the essentials of a full-blooded derby?

Perhaps one of the most unpleasant pills United fans have had to swallow came in the play-offs at the end of the 1989-90 season when Sunderland triumphed over two legs, just when it looked as though the Magpies were likely to make it back into Division One at the first attempt.

With the Keegan-led revival in full spate, United seemed to be taking over top spot in the north-east again when they powered to the old Second Division title in 1992-93 – but, two years on, Middlesbrough also made it to the Premiership. Not to be outdone, Sunderland arrived a year later, bringing the promise of some seriously competitive football to their corner of Britain. Mixed fortunes awaited the trio, Newcastle finishing runners-up in two successive seasons as their rivals took the drop at the end of the 1996-97 campaign.

As a final point, United probably played their longest game ever in a local derby – the Tyne-Tees Cup Final of 1944 versus Darlington, decided by a Milburn goal after 147 minutes. Played over two legs, the aggregate score after extra time had been 3-3, so a decision was taken to let the game be decided by the first goal to be scored. And Wor Jackie did it!

Through The Years
March

1901
March
18

Goalkeeper Matt Kingsley became the first Newcastle player to appear in a full international when England faced Wales. This 6-0 win was to be his only international appearance.

1902
March
1

Jock Rutherford, at only 17 years and 139 days old, became the youngest player ever to score for United's first team in the 4-1 home win over Bolton Wanderers. The record still stands today.

1908
March
28

United, the reigning League Champions, faced giantkilling upstarts Fulham in the FA Cup Semi-Final at Anfield. It turned out to be an unequal contest as the Tynesiders ran out easy 6-0 winners, the margin being the highest ever for the Semi-Final round.

1969
March
26

A time for celebration at St James' Park as Vitoria Setubal were beaten over two legs in the Inter-Cities Fairs Cup, giving United a Semi-Final place.

1974
March
9

The FA Cup Quarter-Final tie against Nottingham Forest, won 4-3 by United, was ordered to be replayed after a pitch invasion took place. United won through after two replays at Goodison Park, thanks to a lone goal by Malcolm Macdonald. Supermac also scored both goals in the Semi-Final defeat of Burnley *en route* to a Wembley date with Liverpool.

1994
March
24

United shattered their transfer record when they signed Darren Peacock from Queens Park Rangers for £2.7 million – though this sum would seem a relative drop in the ocean only a few years later. Perhaps just as significantly, Peter Beardsley was winning his 50th England cap against Denmark, fulfilling a prediction by manager Kevin Keegan that he would revive his international career with a move to Tyneside.

FA CUP RECORD

The quest for England's premier knockout trophy has created over a century of fixtures – all documented here.

Stage	Opponents	Score
	1892-93	
Round 1	Middlesbrough	2-3
	1893-94	
Round 1	Sheffield United	2-0
Round 2	Bolton Wanderers	1-2
	1894-95	
Round 1	Burnley	2-1
Round 2	Aston Villa	1-7
	1895-96	
Prelim	Leadgate Exiles	Walkover
Qualifier 1	W Hartlepool NER	8-0
Qualifier 2	Middlesbrough	4-1
Qualifier 3	Rendel	5-0
Qualifier 4	Tow Law Town	4-0
Round 1	Chesterfield	4-0
Round 2	Bury	1-3
	1896-97	
Round 1	Aston Villa	0-5

Stage	Opponents	Score
1897-98		
Qualifier 3	Willington Athletic	6-0
Qualifier 4	Stockton	4-1
Qualifier 5	Middlesbrough	2-0
Round 1	Preston North End	2-1
Round 2	Southampton St Mary's	0-1
1898-99		
Round 1	Glossop	1-0
Round 2	Liverpool	1-3
1899-1900		
Round 1	Reading	2-1
Round 2	Southampton	*0-0, 1-4
** Match abandoned after 50 minutes*		
1900-01		
Round 1	Middlesbrough	1-3
1901-02		
Round 1	Woolwich Arsenal	2-0
Round 2	Sunderland	1-0
Round 3	Sheffield United	1-1, 1-2
1902-03		
Round 1	Grimsby Town	1-2
1903-04		
Round 1	Bury	1-2

Stage	Opponents	Score
1904-05		
Round 1	Plymouth Argyle	1-1, 1-1, 2-0
Round 2	Tottenham Hotspur	1-1, 4-0
Quarter-Final	Bolton Wanderers	2-0
Semi-Final	Sheffield Wednesday	1-0
Final	Aston Villa	0-2
1905-06		
Round 1	Grimsby Town	6-0
Round 2	Derby County	0-0, 2-1
Round 3	Blackpool	5-0
Quarter-Final	Birmingham	2-2, 3-0
Semi-Final	Woolwich Arsenal	2-0
Final	Everton	0-1
1906-07		
Round 1	Crystal Palace	0-1
1907-08		
Round 1	Nottingham Forest	2-0
Round 2	West Ham United	2-0
Round 3	Liverpool	3-1
Quarter-Final	Grimsby Town	5-1
Semi-Final	Fulham	6-0
Final	Wolverhampton W	1-3
1908-09		
Round 1	Clapton Orient	5-0
Round 2	Blackpool	2-1
Round 3	West Ham United	0-0, 2-1
Quarter-Final	Sunderland	2-2, 3-0
Semi-Final	Manchester United	0-1

Stage	Opponents	Score
1909-10		
Round 1	Stoke	1-1, 2-1
Round 2	Fulham	4-0
Round 3	Blackburn Rovers	3-1
Quarter-Final	Leicester Fosse	3-0
Semi-Final	Swindon Town	2-0
Final	Barnsley	1-1, 2-0
1910-11		
Round 1	Bury	6-1
Round 2	Northampton Town	1-1, 1-0
Round 3	Hull City	3-2
Quarter-Final	Derby County	4-0
Semi-Final	Chelsea	3-0
Final	Bradford City	0-0, 0-1
1911-12		
Round 1	Derby County	0-3
1912-13		
Round 1	Bradford City	*1-0, 1-0
** Match abandoned after 45 minutes*		
Round 2	Hull City	0-0, 3-0
Round 3	Liverpool	1-1, 1-0
Quarter-Final	Sunderland	0-0, 2-2, 0-3
1913-14		
Round 1	Sheffield United	0-5

Stage	Opponents	Score
1914-15		
Round 1	West Ham United	2-2, 3-2
Round 2	Swansea Town	1-1, 2-0
Round 3	Sheffield Wednesday	2-1
Quarter-Final	Chelsea	1-1, 0-1
1919-20		
Round 1	Crystal Palace	2-0
Round 2	Huddersfield Town	0-1
1920-21		
Round 1	Nottingham Forest	1-1, 2-0
Round 2	Liverpool	1-0
Round 3	Everton	0-3
1921-22		
Round 1	Newport County	6-0
Round 2	Preston North End	1-3
1922-23		
Round 1	Southampton	0-0, 1-3
1923-24		
Round 1	Portsmouth	4-2
Round 2	Derby County	2-2, 2-2, 2-2, 5-3
Round 3	Watford	1-0
Quarter-Final	Liverpool	1-0
Semi-Final	Manchester City	2-0
Final	Aston Villa	2-0
1924-25		
Round 1	Hartlepools United	4-1
Round 2	Leicester City	2-2, 0-1

Stage	Opponents	Score
1925-26		
Round 3	Aberdare Athletic	4-1
Round 4	Cardiff City	2-0
Round 5	Clapton Orient	0-2
1926-27		
Round 3	Notts County	8-1
Round 4	Corinthians	3-1
Round 5	Southampton	1-2
1927-28		
Round 3	Blackburn Rovers	1-4
1928-29		
Round 3	Swindon Town	0-2
1929-30		
Round 3	York City	1-1, 2-1
Round 4	Clapton Orient	3-1
Round 5	Brighton & HA	3-0
Quarter-Final	Hull City	1-1, 0-1
1930-31		
Round 3	Nottingham Forest	4-0
Round 4	Leeds United	1-4
1931-32		
Round 3	Blackpool	1-1, 1-0
Round 4	Southport	1-1, 1-1, 9-0
Round 5	Leicester City	3-1
Quarter-Final	Watford	5-0
Semi-Final	Chelsea	2-1
Final	Arsenal	2-1

Stage	Opponents	Score
	1932-33	
Round 3	Leeds United	0-3
	1933-34	
Round 3	Wolverhampton W	0-1
	1934-35	
Round 3	Hull City	5-1
Round 4	Tottenham Hotspur	0-2
	1935-36	
Round 3	Walsall	2-0
Round 4	Sheffield Wednesday	1-1, 3-1
Round 5	Arsenal	3-3, 0-3
	1936-37	
Round 3	Preston North End	0-2
	1937-38	
Round 3	West Bromwich Albion	0-1
	1938-39	
Round 3	Brentford	2-0
Round 4	Cardiff City	0-0, 4-1
Round 5	Preston North End	1-2
	1945-46	
Round 3	Barnsley	4-2, 0-3

Stage	Opponents	Score
1946-47		
Round 3	Crystal Palace	6-2
Round 4	Southampton	3-1
Round 5	Leicester City	1-1, 2-1
Quarter-Final	Sheffield United	2-0
Semi-Final	Charlton Athletic	0-4
1947-48		
Round 3	Charlton Athletic	1-2
1948-49		
Round 3	Bradford Park Avenue	0-2
1949-50		
Round 3	Oldham Athletic	7-2
Round 4	Chelsea	0-3
1950-51		
Round 3	Bury	4-1
Round 4	Bolton Wanderers	3-2
Round 5	Stoke City	4-2
Quarter-Final	Bristol Rovers	0-0, 3-1
Semi-Final	Wolverhampton W	0-0, 2-1
Final	Blackpool	2-0
1951-52		
Round 3	Aston Villa	4-2
Round 4	Tottenham Hotspur	3-0
Round 5	Swansea Town	1-0
Quarter-Final	Portsmouth	4-2
Semi-Final	Blackburn Rovers	0-0, 2-1
Final	Arsenal	1-0

Stage	Opponents	Score
1952-53		
Round 3	Swansea Town	*0-0, 3-0
** Match abandoned after eight minutes*		
Round 4	Rotherham United	1-3
1953-54		
Round 3	Wigan Athletic	2-2, 3-2
Round 4	Burnley	1-1, 1-0
Round 5	West Bromwich Albion	2-3
1954-55		
Round 3	Plymouth Argyle	1-0
Round 4	Brentford	3-2
Round 5	Nottingham Forest	1-1, 2-2, 2-1
Quarter-Final	Huddersfield Town	1-1, 2-0
Semi-Final	York City	1-1, 2-0
Final	Manchester City	3-1
1955-56		
Round 3	Sheffield Wednesday	3-1
Round 4	Fulham	5-4
Round 5	Stoke City	2-1
Quarter-Final	Sunderland	0-2
1956-57		
Round 3	Manchester City	1-1, 5-4
Round 4	Millwall	1-2
1957-58		
Round 3	Plymouth Argyle	6-1
Round 4	Scunthorpe United	1-3

Stage	Opponents	Score
	1958-59	
Round 3	Chelsea	1-4
	1959-60	
Round 3	Wolverhampton W	2-2, 2-4
	1960-61	
Round 3	Fulham	5-0
Round 4	Stockport County	4-0
Round 5	Stoke City	3-1
Quarter-Final	Sheffield United	1-3
	1961-62	
Round 3	Peterborough United	0-1
	1962-63	
Round 3	Bradford City	6-1
Round 4	Norwich City	0-5
	1963-64	
Round 3	Bedford Town	1-2
	1964-65	
Round 3	Swansea Town	0-1
	1965-66	
Round 3	Chester	3-1
Round 4	Sheffield Wednesday	1-2
	1966-67	
Round 3	Coventry City	4-3
Round 4	Nottingham Forest	0-3

Stage	Opponents	Score
1967-68		
Round 3	Carlisle United	0-1
1968-69		
Round 3	Reading	4-0
Round 4	Manchester City	0-0, 0-2
1969-70		
Round 3	Southampton	0-3
1970-71		
Round 3	Ipswich Town	1-1, 1-2
1971-72		
Round 3	Hereford United	2-2, 1-2
1972-73		
Round 3	Bournemouth	2-0
Round 4	Luton Town	0-2
1973-74		
Round 3	Hendon	1-1, 4-0
Round 4	Scunthorpe United	1-1, 3-0
Round 5	West Bromwich Albion	3-0
Quarter-Final	Nottingham Forest	*4-3, 0-0, 1-0
** A replay was ordered by the FA following a pitch invasion*		
Semi-Final	Burnley	2-0
Final	Liverpool	0-3
1974-75		
Round 3	Manchester City	2-0
Round 4	Walsall	0-1

Stage	Opponents	Score
1975-76		
Round 3	Queens Park Rangers	0-0, 2-1
Round 4	Coventry City	1-1, 5-0
Round 5	Bolton Wanderers	3-3, 0-0, 2-1
Quarter-Final	Derby County	2-4
1976-77		
Round 3	Sheffield United	0-0, 3-1
Round 4	Manchester City	1-3
1977-78		
Round 3	Peterborough United	1-1, 2-0
Round 4	Wrexham	2-2, 1-4
1978-79		
Round 3	Torquay United	3-1
Round 4	Wolverhampton W	1-1, 0-1
1979-80		
Round 3	Chester	0-2
1980-81		
Round 3	Sheffield Wednesday	2-1
Round 4	Luton Town	2-1
Round 5	Exeter City	1-1, 0-4
1981-82		
Round 3	Colchester United	1-1, 4-3
Round 4	Grimsby Town	1-2
1982-83		
Round 3	Brighton & HA	1-1, 0-1

NEWCASTLE

Stage	Opponents	Score
	1983-84	
Round 3	Liverpool	0-4
	1984-85	
Round 3	Nottingham Forest	1-1, 1-3
	1985-86	
Round 3	Brighton & HA	0-2
	1986-87	
Round 3	Northampton Town	2-1
Round 4	Preston North End	2-0
Round 5	Tottenham Hotspur	0-1
	1987-88	
Round 3	Crystal Palace	1-0
Round 4	Swindon Town	5-0
Round 5	Wimbledon	1-3
	1988-89	
Round 3	Watford	0-0, 2-2, 0-0, 0-1
	1989-90	
Round 3	Hull City	1-0
Round 4	Reading	3-3, 4-1
Round 5	Manchester United	2-3
	1990-91	
Round 3	Derby County	2-0
Round 4	Nottingham Forest	2-2, 0-3

Stage	Opponents	Score
1991-92		
Round 3	Bournemouth	0-0, *0-0, 2-2
	** Match abandoned after 17 minutes*	
	Newcastle lost 3-4 on penalties	
1992-93		
Round 3	Port Vale	4-0
Round 4	Rotherham United	1-1, 2-0
Round 5	Blackburn Rovers	0-1
1993-94		
Round 3	Coventry City	1-0
Round 4	Luton Town	1-1, 0-2
1994-95		
Round 3	Blackburn Rovers	1-1, 2-1
Round 4	Swansea City	3-0
Round 5	Manchester City	3-1
Quarter-Final	Everton	0-1
1995-96		
Round 3	Chelsea	1-1, 2-2
	Newcastle lost 2-4 on penalties	
1996-97		
Round 3	Charlton Athletic	1-1, 2-1
Round 4	Nottingham Forest	1-2

FA Cup Record Club By Club

Opposition	P	W	D	L	F-A
Aberdare Athletic	1	1	—	—	4-1
Arsenal	6	4	1	1	10-7
Aston Villa	5	2	—	3	7-16
Barnsley	4	2	1	1	7-6
Bedford Town	1	—	—	1	1-2
Birmingham City	2	1	1	—	5-2
Blackburn Rovers	7	3	2	2	9-9
Blackpool	5	4	1	—	11-2
Bolton Wanderers	6	3	2	1	11-8
Bournemouth	3	1	2	—	4-2
Bradford City	4	2	1	1	7-2
Bradford Park Avenue	1	—	—	1	0-2
Brentford	2	2	—	—	5-2
Brighton & HA	4	1	1	2	4-4
Bristol Rovers	2	1	1	—	3-1
Burnley	4	3	1	—	6-2
Bury	4	2	—	2	12-7
Cardiff City	3	2	1	—	6-1
Carlisle United	1	—	—	1	0-1
Charlton Athletic	4	1	1	2	4-8
Chelsea	8	2	3	3	10-13
Chester	2	1	—	1	3-3
Chesterfield	1	1	—	—	4-0
Colchester United	2	1	1	—	5-4
Corinthians	1	1	—	—	3-1
Coventry City	4	3	1	—	11-4
Crystal Palace	4	3	—	1	9-3
Derby County	10	4	4	2	21-17
Everton	3	—	—	3	0-5
Exeter City	2	—	1	1	1-5
Fulham	4	4	—	—	20-4
Glossop	1	1	—	—	1-0
Grimsby Town	4	2	—	2	13-5
W Hartlepool NER	1	1	—	—	8-0
Hartlepool United	1	1	—	—	4-1
Hendon	2	1	1	—	5-1
Hereford United	2	—	1	1	3-4
Huddersfield Town	3	1	1	1	3-2
Hull City	7	4	2	1	13-5
Ipswich Town	2	—	1	1	2-3
Leeds United	2	—	—	2	1-7
Leicester City	6	3	2	1	11-6

Leyton Orient	3	2	—	1	8-3
Liverpool	8	4	1	3	8-12
Luton Town	4	1	1	2	3-6
Manchester City	9	5	2	2	17-12
Manchester United	2	—	—	2	2-4
Middlesbrough	4	2	—	2	9-7
Millwall	1	—	—	1	1-2
Newport County	1	1	—	—	6-0
Northampton Town	3	2	1	—	4-2
Norwich City	1	—	—	1	0-5
Nottingham Forest	15	5	6	4	20-19
Notts County	1	1	—	—	8-1
Oldham Athletic	1	1	—	—	7-2
Peterborough United	3	1	1	1	3-2
Plymouth Argyle	5	3	2	—	11-3
Port Vale	1	1	—	—	4-0
Portsmouth	2	2	—	—	8-4
Preston North End	5	2	—	3	6-8
Queens Park Rangers	2	1	1	—	2-1
Reading	4	3	1	—	13-5
Rendel	1	1	—	—	5-0
Rotherham United	3	1	1	1	4-4
Scunthorpe United	3	1	1	1	5-4
Sheffield United	8	3	2	3	10-12
Sheffield Wednesday	7	5	1	1	13-7
Southampton	7	1	1	5	6-14
Southport	3	1	2	—	11-2
Stockport County	1	1	—	—	4-0
Stockton	1	1	—	—	4-1
Stoke City	5	4	1	—	12-6
Sunderland	7	2	3	2	8-9
Swansea City	6	4	1	1	10-2
Swindon Town	3	2	—	1	7-2
Torquay United	1	1	—	—	3-1
Tottenham Hotspur	5	2	1	2	8-4
Tow Law Town	1	1	—	—	4-0
Walsall	2	1	—	1	2-1
Watford	6	2	3	1	8-3
West Bromwich Albion	3	1	—	2	5-4
West Ham United	5	3	2	—	9-5
Wigan Athletic	2	1	1	—	5-4
Willington Athletic	1	1	—	—	6-0
Wimbledon	1	—	—	1	1-3
Wolves	8	1	3	4	8-13
Wrexham	2	—	1	1	3-6
York City	4	2	2	—	6-3

Cream Of The Continent

Players from overseas were a rare breed in English football when United signed George Robledo and his brother Ted from Barnsley in 1949.

They had arrived in England with their family in 1932, after unrest in their native Chile and settled in Yorkshire. Although Ted never made a great impact on Tyneside, George became a great favourite and was the club's leading scorer in his final two seasons at St James' Park. He appeared for Chile on three occasions in the 1950 World Cup in Brazil, including the game against England. At the end of 1952-53, the brothers returned to their home country to play for the Santiago based Colo Colo. George eventually turned to coaching and died in Chile in 1989.

The coming of another South American, Mirandinha, to Newcastle in August 1987 generated great publicity and engendered much excitement at the club. He became the first Brazilian to play in the Football League and had arrived from the Palmeiras club with an impressive goalscoring record, which it was hoped would be carried over into English football. Alas this gamble never came off, for he became an expensive misfit, his undoubted skill never realising its full potential in an ordinary United side which slid into Division Two in 1988-89. Having scored 23 goals in 63 games, he inevitably returned to Brazil and Palmeiras in February 1990, United's selling price being considerably less than their outlay.

In the 1990s, the purchase of foreign players has become

commonplace since Czech goalkeeper Pavel Srnicek was snapped up from Banik Ostrava in January 1991. The goalkeeping position has been a problem area throughout the decade and Srnicek has had a constant battle to retain his place, initially facing competition from both Tommy Wright and Mark Hooper and more recently from Shaka Hislop and Shay Given. But he was still regarded as an important member of the first-team squad at the start of the 1997-98 season.

Kevin Keegan's managership heralded the start of an influx of overseas players. He acquired the services of Belgian international Philippe Albert for over £2.5 million as 1994-95 commenced and played him alongside Swiss international defender Marc Hottiger.

Adding a taste of the exotic was Faustino Asprilla, the Colombian with crowd-pleasing skills who would add the extra flair which United fans had come to expect over the years. Despite single-handedly demolishing Barcelona with a hat-trick in the 1997-98 European Cup, Asprilla found his time at the club riddled with controversy and frustration, in many ways a mirror of the Mirandinha stay, and was happy to return to Parma (the club from which he'd been signed) in January 1998.

His ability was not always matched by application, and for considerable periods during a game it was easy to forget he was part of the United line-up. His devotees argued that the fleeting moments of sheer brilliance were worth the wait and he was unfortunate in being struck down by a serious injury, just at the time the club had been deprived of Alan Shearer's services, when he could have made the striker's role his own

As 1997-98 continued, United were looking to striker Jon Dahl Tomasson and talented, shaven-headed midfielder Georgian Temuri Ketsbaia for inspiration, Italian Alessandro Pistone having settled into a defensive role behind them. Adopted Geordies they may have been, but anyone giving their all was sure of support from the Gallowgate faithful.

Through The Years
April

1905
April
29

United clinched the First Division Championship for the first time, as they defeated North-East rivals Middlesbrough 3-0 on the last day of the season.

1932
April
23

Jack Allen scored twice in the FA Cup win over Arsenal. The game will always be recalled as the 'over the line' Final, as many claimed that Jimmy Richardson's cross for Newcastle's first goal had been made after the ball had crossed the by-line. Allen scored a total of seven goals in the last four rounds of the competition.

1955
April

Thanks to an FA Cup run which involved ten games, the Magpies were forced to play 11 League games in the month, amazingly losing only two.

1965
April
24

Promotion to Division 1 was secured with a 0-0 draw against Manchester City at St James' – the tenth consecutive League game the Magpies had played without defeat.

1985
April
13

Paul Gascoigne made his first-team debut, coming off the bench in a 1-0 win over Queens Park Rangers. The gifted midfielder, then just 17, would have to wait until the start of the next season to gain a regular place.

1994
April
27

Andy Cole claimed the club's goalscoring record with his 40th strike of the season, against Aston Villa. Cole, signed from Bristol City in March 1993 for £1.75 million, was named the PFA Young Player of the Season after his successful top-flight campaign.

20 Things You Probably Never Knew...

1 Bill Appleyard, a United favourite in the century's first decade, had plied his trade as a fisherman, acquiring the nicknames of 'Cockles' and 'Muscles', the latter more appropriate given his physique. He also had an aptitude for other ball games as he won the footballers' billiards championship.

2 Among his many goalscoring records, Hughie Gallagher also has the distinction of having scored the fastest century of goals for United. He only needed three and a half seasons to complete the feat between 1925 and 1927. During this time he also recorded five hat-tricks in one season, 1926-27.

3 A number of games not involving United have taken part at St James' Park, including four full internationals and seven Football League fixtures. Famous amateur sides like Bishop Auckland, Crook Town and Blyth Spartans, appeared in FA Amateur Cup ties and various representative games at lower levels have been held at the venue.

4 East End, the forerunners of Newcastle United, were formed when Stanley Cricket Club decided to set up a football side. Originally called Stanley, it was not long before they became known as East End FC.

5 Alf McMichael, for so many years the club's 'Mr Reliable', holds the dubious distinction of scoring United's fastest ever own-goal. The away game at West Bromwich Albion was only 32 seconds old when he put the ball into his own net.

6 Though his combined fees have totalled several millions, Paul Gascoigne is one of many footballers who have joined League football as a YTS trainee.

7 Len Shackleton, a great non-conformist, often found himself at odds with the game's administrators. In his autobiography, the chapter entitled 'What The Average Director Knows About Football' simply had a blank page.

8 In United's promotion season of 1947-48, the crowds flocked to St James' Park at a staggering average of 56,299 per game, topping 60,000 five times. The following campaign, the average home gate dipped to 53,702 even though First Division football was on offer. The former figure stood as a League record until 1967-68.

9 Perhaps the unluckiest United player to miss out on the glory days at St James' Park was striker Imre Varadi, who in two seasons scored over 40 goals. He registered one more than Kevin Keegan in 1982-83 but Arthur Cox regarded them as incompatible, transferring Varadi to Sheffield Wednesday in August 1983.

10 It was pretty obvious why United wanted the much-admired Hughie Gallagher when you realise that, in his last two seasons at Airdrie, he scored 65 times in 66 games.

11 As well as notching 55 goals in 70 League games for the Magpies, Andy Cole hit 108 goals in his first 197 League games.

12 In 1950–51 United's team of all talents won the FA Cup, but many felt that the Double could have been theirs. Given the firepower they had up front, it's difficult to fathom how they only managed to score eight times in the last 11 League games – and three came in one match.

13 In 1974–75 Malcolm Macdonald scored 27 League and Cup goals, confirming his status as a deadly finisher. The remarkable fact is that he went ten straight League games without scoring at all.

14 Newcastle United's predecessors East End were no strangers to games involving double-figure scores. Alongside two or three 10-goal hauls stands the 19 compiled against Point Pleasant in a local cup tie.

15 Charlie Mitten was one manager who had the nerve in previous decades to alter the design of the Magpies strip, a move greeted by much derision on the terraces. In the present age, when teams can change their strips at the drop of a hat, Mitten would have been in his element.

16 Ex-manager Jack Charlton is not the only United supremo to have managed the Republic of Ireland. Duggie Livingstone, manager between 1954 and 1956, filled the post before arriving in the north-east. Livingstone had a cosmopolitan outlook for the time, coaching Sparta Rotterdam and also managing Belgium.

17 A number of ex-players have spent over 40 years at St James' Park. Joe Richardson, Andy McCombie and Benny Craig all hung up their boots to become club trainer. Stan Seymour completed nearly 50 years in the club's employ and Alex Mutch, who took up the trainer's position in the early 1920s, only retired in the mid-1980s.

18 In 1893 United started a game against Middlesbrough with only ten men and ended a game versus Sheffield United in 1914 with only eight, due to injuries.

19 Wyn Davies broke the mould when retiring from football; instead of going into pub management he became a baker in Bolton, one of his old stamping grounds.

20 United have used as many as 35 players in a season on two occasions, in 1977-78 and 1988-89; in both instances, relegation resulted after disruption caused by managerial changes.

For Club And Country

A number of pre-World War One United sides were packed with international players, including the 1910 FA Cup Final-winning team which had nine capped players. The entire 11 eventually won caps during their Newcastle days.

The first United player to appear for any of the home countries in a full international was goalkeeper Matt Kingsley, who played for England in March 1901, although full-back Bob Foyers had gained a cap for Scotland in 1894 while with a former club. In the same year as Kingsley's breakthrough, centre-half Andy Aitken became the club's first Scottish international. Four years later another full-back, Bill McCracken, claimed the honour of being United's Irish debutant, but it was 1928 before St James' Park sported a Welsh international in the shape of Tom Evans.

Although many United players have won England caps, few have managed to establish themselves as automatic selections. Even the great Jackie Milburn, who seemed to have gained himself a regular spot from 1949 onwards, only appeared twice for his country between 1952 and 1956, despite fine club performances. His ten goals in only 13 appearances, including a debut goal versus Scotland, still makes impressive reading.

Malcolm Macdonald scored six goals in consecutive games against West Germany and Cyprus respectively in 1975: the five against Cyprus was a Wembley record for a full international, but these were the only successful strikes of his England career. The England management never did quite get to grips with how best to use his undoubted pace and power.

Top of the pile when it comes to the winning of England caps in Magpies colours is Peter Beardsley who, in his two stints at the club, won 24 caps in addition to the 35 accumulated in Liverpool colours. Of the current side John Barnes has 79 appearances to his credit, all won before arriving on Tyneside, and Alan Shearer totals 35, seven as a Newcastle player. Kevin Keegan had 63 internationals under his belt prior to becoming a Magpie, Chris Waddle amassed 62 caps (54 post-United) and Paul Gascoigne had 51 as the 1997-98 season got under way, although he had a collection of 13 Under-21 caps before departing St James' Park.

Most capped England players while wearing Newcastle United colours (to start of 1997-98):

Player	Caps
Peter Beardsley	24
Malcolm Macdonald	14
Robert Lee	13
Jackie Milburn	13
Jackie Rutherford	11
David Batty	9
Chris Waddle	8

Hughie Gallagher remains one of United's most famous Scottish internationals, carrying his remarkable goalscoring record into the higher realms of the game. In total he played 20 times for his country between 1924 and 1935, 13 of those appearances coming while in Magpie colours, notching 23 goals in the process, including five against Northern Ireland plus a couple of hat-tricks.

Roy Aitken has the distinction of being the most capped Scot to play for the black and whites, but only six of his 57 games were during his stay at St James' Park. His namesake Andy Aitken, who also captained his home country, lined up

14 times in the dark blue shirt, his appearances spread over his time at United, Middlesbrough and Leicester Fosse. For part of his international career the latter Aitken was joined by United's Peter McWilliam who played his final game in 1911, when he received the serious injury which finished his career.

Sixty years later, Bobby Moncur emulated Aitken by becoming Scotland's captain in his sixth game out of the 16 he appeared in between 1968 and 1972.

Most capped Scotland players while wearing Newcastle United colours (to start of 1997-98):

Player	Caps
Bobby Moncur	16
Hughie Gallagher	13
Andy Aitken	8
Peter McWilliam	7
Roy Aitken	6

Welshman Ivor Allchurch MBE will always be one of United's best known international players, generally admired throughout all levels of the game and a model to schoolboys with a passion for football. His creative and goalscoring skills were tailor-made for the international stage and for many years he held the distinction of being his country's most capped player. From 1951 to his final match in 1966 against England he made 68 appearances, scoring 23 goals. Up to the 1997-98 season only Ian Rush, who brought his talents to St James' Park for that campaign, had surpassed that total for the Principality.

When signing for United from Swansea, Ivor had already gained 35 caps and collected his MBE. During his four seasons in the black and white stripes he added a further 14 appearances, which were topped up when moving back to Wales. He could still be seen playing minor-league football at 50 years of age.

After Allchurch, Wyn Davies is the highest-profile United player to perform for Wales, collecting 34 caps, 11 with the

Geordies. Only seven goals came his way but, as at club level, 'Wyn the Leap' caused opposing centre-halves all kinds of problems. Davies also won international recognition in his days at Bolton, Manchester City, Manchester United and Blackpool.

Billy Foulkes (not to be confused with Manchester United's Bill Foulkes), who made nearly 70 appearances for the Magpies, made an immediate impact on the international scene, scoring on his debut. Both he and Dave Hollins were actually capped during their time in United's reserves.

Most capped Wales players while wearing Newcastle United colours (to start of 1997-98):

Player	Caps
Ivor Allchurch	14
Wyn Davies	11
Billy Foulkes	11
Dave Hollins	11
Ollie Burton	7
Reg Davies	6

Irishman Billy McCracken was one of United's earliest and most controversial international players, his mastery of the offside trap failing to endear him to a number of his contemporaries. Both on and off the pitch he seemed to be constantly in dispute with the game's authorities, including an argument over payments for international games, and this limited the number of Northern Ireland caps he won. Records suggest he made either 15 or 17 appearances for his country (eight as a Newcastle player) but, whatever the total, McCracken's honours were won in the early part of the century when there was a single Irish side.

Another who captained his country was Alf McMichael, his 40 Northern Ireland caps between 1950 and 1960 constituting a club record. With club colleagues Dick Keith and Tommy Casey, McMichael appeared in the 1958 World Cup Finals, the full-backs playing together 12 times in total.

Two players who should have received many more caps than they did are David Craig and Willie McFaul, for totally different reasons. Craig would probably have substantially passed McMichael's total had injuries not taken a hand, while goalkeeper McFaul doesn't enter the 'most capped' list because of the consistency of Pat Jennings.

David McCreery, a stalwart of the the United sides in the 1980s, was already an established international when arriving in the north-east and continued to appear on the world stage, including the 1986 World Cup Final. Tommy Wright was still adding to his total in 1997 and Keith Gillespie has established himself as one of the mainstays of the Northern Ireland side as they try to overcome a spell in the doldrums.

Most capped Northern Ireland players while wearing Newcastle United colours (to start of 1997-98):

Player	Caps
Alf McMichael	40
David Craig	25
Dick Keith	23
Tommy Cassidy	20
David McCreery	19
Tommy Wright	16
Keith Gillespie	14

When it comes to international football in Eire, Newcastle United can claim to have supplied the most successful manager in the Republic's history – Jack Charlton, who took on the job six months after walking out of St James's disillusioned by the fans' treatment of him. Ironically, it was his close rapport with the Irish following that would help cement his legend.

Despite the Charlton connection, Newcastle's Eire internationals have been few and far between in any era. Liam Tuohy, an outside-left purchased from Shamrock Rovers who played 38 League games for the club between 1960 and 1962, was the first, making three appearances in that final season, two against that footballing giant Iceland. We then have to wait 17 years for midfielder Mick Martin, who joined the Magpies from West Bromwich having already played for Bohemians and Manchester United. He'd win 51 caps for his country, 22 of which came while at St James'.

Another midfielder, John Anderson, served United well between 1982 and 1990 and clocked up 11 Eire caps during that time. His last came in 1989, the same year Liam O'Brien made his international bow versus Spain. He'd partially followed Mick Martin's route to St James', via Bohemians and Manchester United, but would end up at Tranmere in the mid 1990s having failed to live up to initial promise.

Goalkeeper Gary Kelly, now of Oldham, played for the Under-21 side in the 1980s, while Shay Given, one of three keepers currently battling it out for the Newcastle first-team shirt, is a regular in today's full national side. He'd made nine full appearances for the Republic by the time he signed for Newcastle from Blackburn Rovers in summer 1997, and many more look in prospect.

Most capped Republic of Ireland players while wearing Newcastle United colours (to start of 1997-98):

Player	Caps
Mick Martin	22
John Anderson	11
Liam Tuohy	3
Liam O'Brien	1

Worst Season 1

Having finished in eighth position at the end of 1959-60, the new campaign promised much despite the departure of George Eastham for Arsenal.

Few alarm bells were ringing as the team started impressively with 3-2 and 7-2 wins over Preston North End and Fulham respectively. Len White clearly still had his goal touch, scoring four in those games as arch-schemer Ivor Allchurch supplied deadly passes. If a few of the players were coming towards the end of their careers, such as Bobby Mitchell and Jimmy Scoular, surely the younger players could step into the breach?

When New Year's Day arrived with only another five wins to celebrate things were clearly going wrong: the defence appeared to be manager Charlie Mitten's biggest problem, conceding three or more on 13 occasions between the end of August and New Year. Scoring goals during that same period was not a problem, for three or more were registered in nine matches. White's ability to score remained the club's lifeline to survival.

A period of 11 games without a win through December to almost the end of February proved to be the crucial factor, United descending to 20th position. The final nail in the coffin came ironically enough in an away win at Tottenham, when Len White was injured after tangling with Dave Mackay. He was not seen again that season and only four goals came United's way in the next six matches.

One week into April and a 4–0 defeat at Everton, plus a reverse at Blackpool, booked United's passage into Division Two, even though the final two League games turned out to be comfortable victories.

This transitional season had resulted in disaster for the Tynesiders and seen final games from Mitchell, Scoular and Stokoe, whose boots had clearly not been filled by others. Four years would pass before United reclaimed their place in the top flight, but Joe Harvey would have to replace Mitten before this could be accomplished.

1960-61 LEAGUE RECORD		
Opponents	**Home**	**Away**
Arsenal	3-3	0-5
Aston Villa	2-1	0-2
Birmingham City	2-2	1-2
Blackburn Rovers	3-1	4-2
Blackpool	4-3	1-2
Bolton Wanderers	4-1	1-2
Burnley	0-1	3-5
Cardiff City	5-0	2-3
Chelsea	1-6	2-4
Everton	0-4	0-5
Fulham	7-2	3-4
Leicester City	1-3	3-5
Manchester City	1-3	3-3
Manchester United	1-1	2-3
Nottingham Forest	2-2	2-0
Preston North End	0-0	3-2
Sheffield Wednesday	0-1	1-1
Tottenham Hotspur	3-4	2-1
West Bromwich Albion	3-2	0-6
West Ham United	5-5	1-1
Wolverhampton Wanderers	4-4	1-2

Double Acts

It is an indisputable fact that great teams thrive on the almost telepathic understanding provided by a dynamic duo, and this is often the difference between success and failure.

The forging of an understanding between players can often take time. Individuals do not always gel as intended and managers repeatedly lose their jobs, not because of a lack of talent in their line-up, but due to lack of cohesion.

An early Magpies duo, full-backs Billy McCracken and Frank Hudspeth, played in a substantial number of games together and prospered under the old offside law. McCracken played for United until he was 40 years of age and Hudspeth was not far short when being transferred in 1929. Hudspeth actually took over the club captaincy from McCracken when the latter left for Hull City in 1923.

Dick Keith and Alf McMichael stand out among later defensive pairings, both for United and their country, their finest hour coming as part of the Northern Ireland side which distinguished itself in the 1958 World Cup in Sweden. For six seasons or more the two became famous for their reliability, the team-sheet seeming incomplete without both names being present. McMichael eventually went into management but Keith sadly died in an accident at only 34 years of age.

One partnership that worked well for United was the two Cs, Clark and Craig, who figured in that famous Fairs Cup victory in 1969. The former was a Northern Ireland international with natural talent not always associated with full-backs, the latter a player whose byword was dependability. It's very likely that both of them will forever stay in the Top 10 list of all-time appearances.

Alan Kennedy and Irving Nattrass were a different type of twosome. Kennedy loved to join the attack, while Nattrass was content in a defensive role. In 1978 the full-back combination was broken up when Kennedy became part of the formidable Liverpool side of the time. Nattrass only lingered a further season before a move to Middlesbrough.

The current side featuring Darren Peacock and Philippe Albert gives the same kind of options as those offered by the Kennedy-Nattrass duo, Albert taking up Kennedy's marauding role. In the side which won the Fairs Cup, there were at least two other double acts crucial to success: Bobby Moncur and Ollie Burton were the central defensive rock upon which victory depended, while up front Bryan Robson and Wyn Davies proved a potent strike force after a bedding-in period. In a little under five seasons together the pair scored 133 goals, the sheer physical presence of Davies allowing Robson space to develop his predatory instincts.

Of the old-style wing-halves few were more successful than Joe Harvey and Charlie Crowe, part of the 1951 Cup-winning team. Crowe was a Newcastle player longer than Harvey, his first-team appearances being hampered by injury over 12 seasons. As captain, Harvey supplied the inspiration for those around him, offering a combination of guile and total commitment. Crowe made up for his lack of finesse by always giving one hundred per cent, constantly harrying the opposition and never allowing them to settle. This kind of balance was also provided by Roddie McKenzie and Willie Gibson, the engine-room of the 1926-27 League Championship side.

In creative terms, United have never fielded two players quite like Ivor Allchurch and George Eastham in the same side. Both were exemplary passers of the ball and, in Len

White, they had a forward who relished the kind of service they could offer.

Apart from laying on chances for others, two seasons saw Allchurch and Eastham score 57 League and Cup goals between them, while in 1959-60 Eastham netted 20 times in 44 starts. What further triumphs these two might have looked forward to in Magpie colours will always remain conjecture, for Eastham left in November 1960 during his dispute with the club; Allchurch departed two seasons later. How significant that United were relegated the season of Eastham's departure.

When it comes to partnerships, both on and off the field, the Kevin Keegan-Terry McDermott relationship is an unique one, helping achieve promotion as players and coming so close to securing the Championship in successive seasons as managers. As a player Keegan benefited from McDermott's midfield probing, while they seemed the perfect combination as a management team, both bent on sending out a side which would play entertaining football in its quest for trophies. Alas, they were never able to realise their ambition.

Returning to forward associations, Mark McGhee and Mick Quinn ran riot in Division Two. The 1989-90 season proved most productive, Quinn scoring 34 goals in 53 games and McGhee 25 in 55. Both had bags of experience under their belts before joining United in the previous close season, McGhee for the second time, and their goals carried the Magpies into the play-offs.

The Malcolm Macdonald-John Tudor relationship is perhaps a less obvious one, Tudor suffering because he wasn't quite the extrovert nor confident character his partner was. He was a selfless player who battled hard in the penalty area, taking a lot of the stick which would have been otherwise meted out to his more illustrious colleague. The two first came together at the start of the 1971-72 season and operated effectively for four years, Macdonald taking most of the glory and Tudor happy to play his part. When Macdonald left Tyneside he had 121 goals to his credit: Tudor had only 58, but many of his partner's strikes were due to his efforts.

Few effective partnerships have yet been established in the current United line-up due to injuries, suspensions and recent departures. Who could have imagined Faustino Asprilla acting in tandem with anybody, anyway? But most Geordies rue the combination that got away – Alan Shearer and Les Ferdinand, a spearhead which only lasted for one season at club level.

Through The Years
May

1944
May

St James' Park was used by the authorities during the Second World War for military training and storage purposes, so nobody should have been surprised when US servicemen were seen to organise a baseball match– not the only time that the playing area has been used for other purposes.

1949
May

United did not appear to take pity on inferior opposition while on an end-of-season North American tour. They scored 25 goals in their first three games, including 13 against Saskatchewan.

1952
May
3

United became the first team since Blackburn Rovers, 60 years before, to retain the FA Cup. George Robledo's single goal being enough to lift the trophy against Arsenal.

1956
May

George Eastham, the cultured midfielder who would be a crucial figure in one of the games most contentious issues, players' freedom of contract, signed for United aged 18.

1969
May
21

United defeated Glasgow Rangers in an acrimonious Inter-Cities Fairs Cup Semi-Final, the second leg being won at home by 2-0 amid bottle-throwing and a pitch invasion by drunken and dejected Rangers fans. The first leg at Ibrox, played before a crowd of 75,580, finished goalless, thanks to Willie McFaul's heroics between the sticks

1997
May
11

The final League game of the season, a 5-0 battering of relegated Nottingham Forest, confirmed the Magpies as runners-up to Manchester United when earlier in the season they had topped the table and looked potential winners. The consolation for many fans was the relegation of both Sunderland and Middlesbrough.

Great Midfielders

Combative and creative players in the middle of the park have played their part in bringing soccer success to Tyneside.

Terry Hibbitt

Hard-working Hibbitt is best remembered as the midfield dynamo who laid on so many chances for Malcolm Macdonald, as the latter became the most feared striker in the Football League. Both he and 'Supermac' made their League debuts on the opening day of the 1971-72 season in a 2-0 defeat at Crystal Palace.

Although United never had much success during his two spells at the club, Hibbitt himself earned a reputation as one of the game's most valued playmakers, his high workrate and sweet left foot never failing to catch the eye. Having spent many years at Leeds United before the move to Tyneside, Hibbitt had been schooled in the toughest of academies, and this obviously worked to United's benefit when the chips were down: when other heads *had* fallen he could always be relied upon to keep things going.

In keeping with most of his colleagues, the disaster of the 1974 FA Cup Final must have been the most disappointing moment of Hibbitt's club career. He did not function on the day, the team simply being swept away contemptuously by a Liverpool side still in second gear.

He lost out on a large piece of the 1974-75 season due to serious injury, but regained his place as the campaign came to a close. He had only played in the first four games of the following season before Gordon Lee sold him to Birmingham City, but the lure of the north-east proved enough to bring him back in 1978.

Bill McGarry made him captain of the newly-relegated side which desperately needed guidance – but as manfully as Hibbitt toiled, United remained in Division Two during his final years, despite looking like possible promotion material in the first half of 1979-80. In 1981, a knee injury forced him out of League football for good, and he died tragically early of cancer, in August 1994 at the age of 46. Brother Kenny, once of Wolves, is currently Cardiff's director of football.

TERRY HIBBITT UNITED RECORD 1971-75, 1978-80

League		FA Cup		League Cup		Europe		Total	
Apps	Goals	Apps	Goals	Apps	Goals	Apps	Goals	Apps	Goals
228	12	15	1	16	—	—	—	259	13

DAVID McCREERY

Like Terry Hibbitt, McCreery was a hundred per center who would keep things ticking over when the going got tough. But there the similarity ends, for his role was that of the midfield iron man who would win the ball for the more creative minds around him. McCreery carried out this function to perfection for Arthur Cox in his promotion side of 1983-84, earning the reputation of a player you would rather have on your side than against you.

McCreery's tackling was always fierce and Keegan, Waddle

and Beardsley benefitted greatly from the combative skills he displayed. His formative years had been spent at Old Trafford, where he had broken into the first team in his teens, but as the years progressed he must have felt his best form was behind him – even though his Northern Ireland place was secure. Queens Park Rangers became a stepping stone to a move to the USA with Tulsa Roughnecks and possible anonymity.

He was rescued in October 1982, a year before Peter Beardsley came back to his homeland from North America, and stepped immediately into the side which Cox was building for better things.

McCreery's performances back in Division One helped stabilise a side recovering from the loss of Keegan and Cox, and he remained a major component in United's line-up until 1989. That year saw the Magpies drop into the Second Division and McCreery accepted a free transfer to Hearts.

His wholehearted approach to the game had given United an extra dimension no team of talented individuals can be without – that element of steel which so often turns matches. David McCreery's popularity at St James' Park shows the fans recognised the part he played in turning round the club's fortunes.

DAVID McCREERY UNITED RECORD 1982-89

League		FA Cup		League Cup		Europe		Total	
Apps	Goals	Apps	Goals	Apps	Goals	Apps	Goals	Apps	Goals
243	2	11	—	15	—	—	—	269	2

Paul Gascoigne

Most followers of the game would agree that witnessing the development of a special talent is one of football's most pleasurable experiences – so what a reward United fans received when 'Gazza' burst on the north-east scene.

His first tentative steps into the first-team came towards the end of the 1984-85 season, the club's first back in the top flight. He needed that spell on the substitutes' bench, but was on the pitch from day one of 1985-86 and really started to make his mark. By May, his natural flair and skilful artistry were being recognised around the country.

Unfortunately, only one season was spent playing alongside Peter Beardsley and Chris Waddle, who had departed before Gascoigne made his mark, so the Geordies were denied the sight of another deadly triumvirate. But his burgeoning talent really needed no assistance, and his ability to go past players at will and his uncanny weight of pass became a talking point.

The first of his 50-plus England caps came in 1989, a year after being named Young Player of The Year – but by then he was no longer a Newcastle player, having been transferred to Tottenham for a national record £2.3 million.

Both at club and international level, he continued to make the headlines, often for non-footballing reasons, and, just as he looked like becoming a Tottenham fixture, Lazio claimed him in 1992 for £5.5 million. After overcoming an injury sustained (thanks to a rash challenge) in his last Spurs game that seemed set to scupper the deal, Gazza's stay in *Serie A* proved to be littered with problems and a move back to the UK and Glasgow Rangers resulted in 1995.

Detractors will tell you of how he has abused his talent by his often impetuous behaviour, while his admirers can easily cite such moments as the spectacular goal against Scotland in Euro '96 to outweigh those actions. The individual traits of Shackleton and Best live on in Paul Gascoigne.

PAUL GASCOIGNE UNITED RECORD 1985-88									
League		FA Cup		League Cup		Europe		Total	
Apps	Goals	Apps	Goals	Apps	Goals	Apps	Goals	Apps	Goals
92	21	4	3	8	1	—	—	104	25

DAVID BATTY

When David Batty's name comes to mind, fans immediately think of a ball-winner who would be welcomed in most clubs for that very quality. United have had their fair share of midfield hard men, even in their most talented sides, so, despite the criticism from some quarters when Kevin Keegan plucked Batty from Blackburn Rovers, it was easy to understand the thinking behind his £3.75 million signing.

Prior to joining Blackburn, Batty had been a regular in the Leeds United side, playing over 200 League games and forging a reputation as a destructive rather than creative performer. The image was very much like that of David McCreery, appreciated by home fans but universally hated elsewhere.

In his autobiography, Keegan openly admits his surprise when he eventually got to know the real Batty, for here was a player he recognised as a true professional, an excellent trainer and one with far more ability than people give him credit for. His one weakness is a lack of goals – only four in the League for Leeds, one in over 50 games at Blackburn and only two in 40-plus games for the Magpies. His sheer determination, one of his greatest assets, should bring him more.

Batty had already become a fixture in the England set up before United went in for him and has quietly accumulated 25 caps since 1991. Kenny Dalglish is also a great admirer of Batty's qualities, and in January 1998 reports were circulating to the effect that the troubled Magpies were offering their midfielder a long-term contract worth £22,000 a week. True or not, this goes a long way to explaining how valuable a property David Batty really is.

DAVID BATTY UNITED RECORD 1996-(97)									
League		FA Cup		League Cup		Europe		Total	
Apps	Goals	Apps	Goals	Apps	Goals	Apps	Goals	Apps	Goals
43	2	3	—	2	—	7	—	55	2

Player Talk

Footballers have brains in their boots – but these Magpie favourites chose to put their thoughts into words.

'I loved Newcastle…until Gordon Lee took over.'
Malcolm Macdonald in 1976, on leaving for Arsenal.

'I maintain that Joe Harvey was only two players away from having a great side.'
Jackie Milburn on the United team of the mid-1970s.

'Everyone was capable of getting in on the act in Keegan's side.' *David McCreery when asked to comment on the merits of various United line-ups in 1994.*

'The worst thing for me was that it was a nothing kind of injury, really. I wouldn't have minded so much if it was a crunching tackle or someone had done me while I'd been trying to score a goal.' *Alan Shearer on his 1997 injury*

'Being turned down by Liverpool was the lowest moment of my life, but it turned out to be a blessing in disguise.'
John Beresford

Not only did Kevin score goals but he had the knack of being there just when you needed him.' *Beardsley on Keegan*

'It didn't take me long to realise that Arthur Cox had unearthed a diamond.' *Keegan on Beardsley*

'I never won anything, so I suppose I was just a workmanlike goalscorer.' *Mick Quinn*

'David Batty and I complement each other in midfield. I've always said that if I had to pick someone to play with it would be David.' *Robert Lee*

'I think it's difficult not to settle in the north-east, because the people here are very friendly.' *Philippe Albert*

'I didn't come her for the culture or the climate, but I want to adapt. I have discovered Newcastle Brown Ale and my ambition is to speak Geordie as well as Peter Beardsley.'
David Ginola

'Joe Harvey used to scream at me if I crossed the half-way line.' *Bobby Moncur*

'Warren Barton's the best-dressed footballer I've ever seen. In training, we're all in tracksuits and he arrives in shirt, trousers and shoes. We call him the Dog, as in the dog's bollocks.'
Robert Lee on a fashion-conscious team-mate

Through The Years
June

1949
June

The Magpies' triumphant North American tour continued with a 16-goal haul against Alberta All Stars and 11 versus Washington State.

1958
June

Having had no manager for two years, United appointed Charlie Mitten to the post, believing him to be just the type of character needed to take the Magpies into the next decade. He did so, but with ever-diminishing success.

1962
June

Joe Harvey took up the post of manager. His tenure lasted 13 years, during which time he turned the club's fortunes around, took them to European glory and secured them a place in the top division.

1963
June

A club record fee for a defender of £37,500 was paid to Norwich for Ollie Burton.

1969
June
11

The Inter-Cities Fairs Cup was clinched in Budapest as a 3-2 victory against Ujpest Dozsa secured the trophy on a 6-2 aggregate. Defender Bobby Moncur, who notched a brace in the Semi-Final, was again among the scorers.

1997
June
7

United's star striker Alan Shearer scored the only goal in England's win over host country France during *Le Tournoi*, a result good enough for England to win the friendly tournament which had also featured Italy and Brazil.

Great Matches

Choosing just six games from over 100 years of a club's history is an impossible task. Listed below is a handful of significant confrontations which can only touch upon United's many glory games.

Newcastle United 7 Aston Villa 5
10 March 1928
League Division One

Twelve goals in a game don't always guarantee football of the highest class, but contemporary reports tell us that this early-spring fixture, played in a mixture of snow showers and brighter periods, really did have everything. This was the second time in the season that Newcastle had scored seven goals, having achieved the feat against Manchester United the previous September. At this juncture, however, Hughie Gallagher was in the middle of a lengthy suspension, and this would be the only League victory the Magpies secured in the space of eight games.

Jonathan 'Monty' Wilkinson, deputising for Gallagher at centre-forward, had a field day, scoring a hat-trick in a game that ebbed and flowed. The home side were four goals to the good after only 30 minutes through Stan Seymour, Tom McDonald, Jock McCurley and Wilkinson, but Villa replied before half-time with goals from Cook and the famed 'Pongo' Waring.

United hit the opposition with another goal burst just over half an hour into the second half, McCurley adding his

second and Wilkinson completing an excellent hat-trick with two more strikes. Seemingly home and dry at 7-2, United had not reckoned with Villa's resilience which produced three goals from Dorrell, York and Waring, despite the visitors having lost their goalkeeper during the mayhem.
Team: Wilson, Maitland, Evans, Harris, Park, Gibson, Urwin, McCurley, Wilkinson, McDonald, Seymour.

Newcastle United 1 Chelsea 0
3 September 1930
League Division One

No selection of best-ever games involving Newcastle could possibly ignore the first home League game of the 1930-31 season which witnessed an early homecoming for Hughie Gallagher, transferred to Chelsea during the summer. This became an emotional occasion for the record crowd, every vantage point being taken, and Gallagher himself quite overcome by the reception he received.

Nobody wished to see their former favourite have a bad game, but every indication is that United's Jack Hill did not give him too much room to turn on the magic, as an under-strength Chelsea side found McInroy difficult to beat. The game looked as though it was drifting to a goalless result, United having been reduced to ten men, when Jackie Cape headed the winner 14 minutes from the end.

Gallagher probably had ambivalent views on the result of the game, but he did regard it as one of the highlights of his career. Returning players often get a hard time from their former supporters but the Scot had attained god-like status at St James' Park; the ecstatic reception he received when taking the field was entirely appropriate.
Team: McInroy, Nelson, Fairhurst, Mathison, Hill, Naylor, Cape, Starling, Lindsay, McDonald, Wilkinson.

Newcastle United 13 Newport County 0
5 October 1946
League Division Two

This game, regarded as one of the most famous massacres in Football League history, came in the middle of an indifferent run for United, being their only win in the space of seven games. The previous home fixture had seen them lose 2-1 to Burnley in front of over 60,000 fans, but this did not deter 50,000-plus turning up for the Newport encounter.

Len Shackleton, just signed from Bradford, ran riot in the first half against a struggling County side recovering from a 7-0 drubbing by West Bromwich Albion. By half time they had conceded a further seven goals against a rampant forward line. Shackleton had grabbed four, including a record-breaking 155-second hat-trick, while Charlie Wayman (who had missed a penalty within the first two minutes) claimed a hat-trick of his own. United scored five of those goals in the space of eight minutes.

The visitors must have thought the worst was over when they came out for the second half but the carnage had only just started. Shackleton scored twice more, the eighth and 13th goal either side of Wayman's fourth, a brace for Milburn and a contribution from Roy Bentley.

Few have witnessed such a complete demolition of a side as Newcastle fans that day, the club recording a new Division Two scoring record and equalling the Football League's highest score. In the 1990s, more cynical fans might look at the scoreline with a certain amount of suspicion, questioning the quality of the opposition – but no one can doubt what a wonderful front five the Magpies had at the time.

Team: Garbutt, Cowell, Graham, Harvey, Brennan, Wright, Milburn, Bentley, Wayman, Shackleton, Pearson.

Newcastle United 2 Inter Milan 0
30 September 1970
Inter-Cities Fairs Cup Final

United were in their third successive season of European competition when drawn against Italian giants Inter Milan who could boast a cast of world-class players, Facchetti and Boninsegna probably being the best remembered. The Fairs Cup had been fairly kind to Newcastle in previous seasons, being winners in 1968-69 and only going out the next season on the away-goals rule.

The two-legged tie had seemed a daunting prospect when the draw was made – but, after leaving Milan with an excellent 1-1 scoreline, the club's confidence had risen dramatically by the second confrontation a week later. United, in inspired mood, took the game to Inter and were a goal up inside half an hour through a Bobby Moncur header. Shortly afterwards a free-for-all developed following a confrontation between Wyn Davies and Inter goalkeeper Vieri. The latter completely lost his head and assaulted the referee, a Mr Minnoy from Belgium, who needed treatment from the United bench.

After the keeper's sending-off, the Italians went to pieces, employing any illegal tactic to make life difficult for United. Indeed the police entered the fray on more than one occasion to calm the situation. The game eventually turned United's way when Davies scored with a diving header for which he received more abuse from the Italians.

Perhaps the game is remembered for the wrong reasons but this was a famous victory over one of the world's great clubs. Inter, on the other hand, left St James' Park having let down both themselves and the game of football.

Team: McFaul, Craig, Clark, Gibb, Burton, Moncur, Robson, Dyson, Davies, Arentoft, Young.

Newcastle United 5 Manchester City 0
29 October 1983
League Division Two

Goals and victories were not uncommon events during the promotion season of 1983-84 but this victory over City is regarded as being as good as anything seen during Keegan's first coming.

This was a game where everything seemed to come together at the same time; the defence rock-solid, McDermott's promptings in midfield paying handsome dividends and the front players only having to enter the final third of the field to look like scoring. Peter Beardsley also chose the game to register a hat-trick, the first by a Newcastle player at St James' Park since Alan Gowling in 1976.

United were a goal up within ten minutes through Beardsley but surprisingly it took until nearly half-time before Keegan added the second from a cross by Waddle. The second 45 minutes found the Magpies playing some devastating football and, on the hour, Beardsley snapped up a rebound from the goalkeeper for number three.

At this stage it was just a matter of how many United would finish with and Beardsley completed his hat-trick in fine fashion as he streaked through the now demoralised City defence. Waddle's shot from outside the penalty area rounded off a superb display which would live long in the memories of the 33,675 United fans who witnessed it.

Team: Thomas, Anderson, Ryan, McCreery, Saunders, Carney, Keegan, Beardsley, Waddle, McDermott, Wharton.

Newcastle United 3 Barcelona 2
17 September 1997
European Cup Group C

Having been hammered 3-1 by Wimbledon in the Premiership four days earlier, and chairman Sir John Hall announcing his retirement, Newcastle went into their clash with mighty Barcelona in chastened mood. Yet such was their command over the Spaniards that a local radio station back home reported 'Barcelona have been destroyed by wave upon wave of Newcastle attacks.' And Faustino Asprilla, that controversial Colombian, was assassin in chief.

A hat-trick in 26 minutes (excluding half-time) sent the Toon Army wild – the first goal coming from the spot on 22 minutes, after keeper Ruud Hesp had brought him crashing down. So cool was the hitman that, having dusted himself off, he re-spotted the ball on the referee's insistence, before strolling back and burying it in the Barcelona net. Tino's second came ten minutes later, Keith Gillespie setting up a gift-wrapped chance for Asprilla to rise above stopper Nadal and banging it into Hesp's top left-hand corner.

The hat-trick was completed three minutes after the break with a second header, suggesting that the injured Alan Shearer was not being missed at all. But just as it all seemed over, gaps appeared at the back, allowing Luis Enrique to put the Spaniards in with a shout. And when, with 88 minutes on the clock, Shay Given fumbled a cross, Warren Barton failed to clear his lines and Luis Figo rammed home the second, Geordie whistles could be heard all the way to the Wear.

The result took the edge off the disappointments of the previous week, leaving Newcastle equal on points at the top of Group C.

Team: Given, Barton, Beresford, Batty, Lee, Barnes (Ketsbaia), Asprilla, Tomasson (Peacock), Gillespie, Watson, Albert.

League Cup Record

Just one Final appearance to date for the Magpies in the 'Junior' Cup competition.

Stage	Opponents	Score
	1960-61	
Round 1	Colchester United	1-4
	1961-62	
Round 1	Scunthorpe United	2-0
Round 2	Sheffield United	2-2, 0-2
	1962-63	
Round 2	Leyton Orient	1-1, 2-4
	1963-64	
Round 2	Preston North End	3-0
Round 3	Bournemouth & Bos Ath	1-2
	1964-65	
Round 2	Blackpool	0-3
	1965-66	
Round 2	Peterborough Unted	3-4
	1966-67	
Round 2	Leeds United	0-1

Stage	Opponents	Score
1967-68		
Round 2	Lincoln City	1-2
1968-69		
Round 2	Southport	2-0
Round 3	Southampton	1-4
1969-70		
Round 2	Sheffield United	0-2
1970-71		
Round 2	Bristol Rovers	1-2
1971-72		
Round 2	Halifax Town	2-1
Round 3	Arsenal	0-4
1972-73		
Round 2	Port Vale	3-1
Round 3	Blackpool	0-3
1973-74		
Round 2	Doncaster Rovers	6-0
Round 3	Birmingham City	2-2, 0-1
1974-75		
Round 2	Nottingham Forest	1-1, 3-0
Round 3	Queens Park Rangers	4-0
Round 4	Fulham	3-0
Quarter-Final	Chester	0-0, 0-1

NEWCASTLE

Stage	Opponents	Score
	1975-76	
Round 2	Southport	6-0
Round 3	Bristol Rovers	1-1, 2-0
Round 4	Queens Park Rangers	3-1
Quarter-Final	Notts County	1-0
Semi-Final	Tottenham Hotspur	0-1, 3-1
Final	Manchester City	1-2
	1976-77	
Round 2	Gillingham	2-1
Round 3	Stoke City	3-0
Round 4	Manchester United	2-7
	1977-78	
Round 2	Millwall	0-2
	1978-79	
Round 2	Watford	1-2
	1979-80	
Round 2	Sunderland	2-2, 2-2
	Newcastle lost on penalties	
	1980-81	
Round 2	Bury	3-2, 0-1
	Newcastle lost on away goals	
	1981-82	
Round 2	Fulham	1-2, 0-2
	1982-83	
Round 2	Leeds United	1-0, 1-4

Stage	Opponents	Score
	1983-84	
Round 2	Oxford United	1-1, 1-2
	1984-85	
Round 2	Bradford City	3-1, 1-0
Round 3	Ipswich Town	1-1, 1-2
	1985-86	
Round 2	Barnsley	0-0, 1-1
	Newcastle won on away goals	
Round 3	Oxford United	1-3
	1986-87	
Round 2	Bradford City	0-2, 1-0
	1987-88	
Round 2	Blackpool	0-1, 4-1
Round 3	Wimbledon	1-2
	1988-89	
Round 2	Sheffield United	0-3, 2-0
	1989-90	
Round 2	Reading	1-3, 4-0
Round 3	West Bromwich Albion	0-1
	1990-91	
Round 2	Middlesbrough	0-2, 1-0
	1991-92	
Round 2	Crewe Alexandra	4-3, 1-0
Round 3	Peterborough United	0-1

Stage	Opponents	Score
1992-93		
Round 1	Mansfield Town	2-1, 0-0
Round 2	Middlesbrough	0-0, 3-1
Round 3	Chelsea	1-2
1993-94		
Round 2	Notts County	4-1, 7-1
Round 3	Wimbledon	1-2
1994-95		
Round 2	Barnsley	2-1, 1-0
Round 3	Manchester United	2-0
Round 4	Manchester City	1-1, 0-2
1995-96		
Round 2	Bristol City	5-0, 3-1
Round 3	Stoke City	4-0
Round 4	Liverpool	1-0
Round 5	Arsenal	0-2
1996-97		
Round 3	Oldham Athletic	1-0
Round 4	Middlesbrough	1-3
1997-98		
Round 3	Hull City	2-0
Round 4	Derby County	1-0
Round 5	Liverpool	0-2

League Cup Record Club By Club

Opposition	P	W	D	L	F-A
Arsenal	2	—	—	2	0-6
Barnsley	4	2	2	—	4-2
Birmingham C	2	—	1	1	2-3
Blackpool	2	—	—	2	0-6
Bournemouth	1	—	—	1	1-2
Bradford C	4	3	—	1	5-3
Bristol C	2	2	—	—	8-1
Bristol R	3	1	1	1	4-3
Bury	2	1	—	1	3-3
Chelsea	1	—	—	1	1-2
Chester	2	—	1	1	0-1
Colchester Utd	1	—	—	1	1-4
Crewe Alex	2	2	—	—	5-3
Derby Co	1	1	—	—	1-0
Doncaster R	1	1	—	—	6-0
Fulham	3	1	—	2	4-4
Gillingham	1	1	—	—	2-1
Halifax T	1	1	—	—	2-1
Hull C	1	1	—	—	2-0
Ipswich T	2	—	1	1	2-3
Leeds U	3	1	—	2	2-5
Leyton Orient	2	—	1	1	3-5
Lincoln C	1	—	—	1	1-2
Liverpool	2	1	—	2	1-2

Opposition	P	W	D	L	F-A
Manchester C	3	—	1	2	2-5
Manchester Utd	2	1	—	1	4-7
Mansfield T	2	1	1	—	2-1
Middlesbrough	5	2	1	2	5-6
Millwall	1	—	—	1	0-2
Nott'm Forest	2	1	1	—	4-1
Notts Co	3	3	—	—	12-2
Oldham Ath	1	1	—	—	1-0
Oxford Utd	3	—	1	2	3-6
Peterboro Utd	2	—	—	2	3-5
Port Vale	1	1	—	—	3-1
Preston NE	1	1	—	—	3-0
QPR	2	2	—	—	7-1
Reading	2	1	—	1	5-3
Scunthorpe Utd	1	1	—	—	2-0
Sheffield Utd	5	1	1	3	4-9
Southampton	1	—	—	1	1-4
Southport	2	2	—	—	8-0
Stoke C	2	2	—	—	7-0
Sunderland	2	—	2	—	4-4
Tottenham H	2	1	—	1	3-2
Watford	1	—	—	1	1-2
West Brom	1	—	—	1	0-1
Wimbledon	2	—	—	2	2-4

The 

Files

The Magpies have always responded to inspirational leadership, both on and off the pitch. Here's a comprehensive list of club managers from 1895 to the present, with ratings out of five.

Frank Watt
1895-1930

Honours:	Division One Champions	1904-05, 1906-07, 1908-09, 1926-27
	FA Cup winners	1909-10, 1923-24
	FA Cup runners-up	1904-05, 1905-06, 1907-08, 1910-11

Watt was not actually designated as team manager, club secretary being his official title, as he guided the club through the early years with a high degree of success. A record of four Division One Championships, two FA Cup wins and four losing Finals helped create the air of expectancy that has long existed at St James' Park.

Andy Cunningham
1930-35
Honours: FA Cup winners 1931-32

Cunningham became not only United's first team manager (as opposed to secretary) in January 1930 but also the first player-manager in the First Division. The Cup win was the highlight of his six seasons at Gallowgate, a rise to fifth place in 1932-33 being followed by relegation the next season.

Tom Mather
1935-39
Honours: None

Mather's stay at Gallowgate saw Newcastle fail to rise from the Second Division: their best position was fourth, the worst a worrying 19th. Unfortunately, he was never able to repeat his performance at Stoke where he took the Division Two Championship in 1933.

Stan Seymour
1939-47 and 1950-54
Honours: FA Cup winners 1950-51, 1951-52

Seymour joined United as a player in 1920 and won both Championship and FA Cup winner's medals before retiring in 1929. Becoming a board member, he took over the team during the difficult war years. In his only proper season the Magpies finished fifth in Division Two and made it to the Cup Semi-Final, losing to Charlton. In his second spell Seymour picked up where predecessor George Martin had left off: United finished in the top half of the table in his first two seasons and the Cup was won in successive years.

George Martin
1947-50
Honours: None

Martin earns his high rating for taking United back into the First Division in his first season and re-establishing the club as a force to be reckoned with in the top flight. High finishes in the next two seasons confirmed the Magpies were in good health, and when Martin left for Villa Park in December 1950, they sat in third place.

Duggie Livingstone
1954-56
Honours: FA Cup winners 1954-55

Livingstone inherited Seymour's team and promptly took it on a successful Cup run. He spent just over a year at St James' Park, being foolhardy enough to drop Jackie Milburn during this period.

Charlie Mitten
1958-61
Honours: None

United had gone two and a half years without a manager (unthinkable in the modern game) prior to appointing Mitten in June 1958. Relatively untried as a manager, the controversial ex-Manchester United winger was probably the flamboyant character the board felt the club needed at the time. Sadly, despite being responsible for assembling the Allchurch, White and Eastham triumvirate, he is best remembered as the man who took the team back to the Second Division in 1961.

Joe Harvey
1962–75

Honours:	Division Two Champions	1964–65
	FA Cup runners-up	1973–74
	Inter-Cities Fairs Cup winners	1968–69
	Texaco Cup winners	1973–74, 1974–75
	Anglo-Italian Cup winners	1972–73

Harvey first joined the Magpies as a player in 1945 and remained as captain for eight years, during which time promotion was achieved and the FA Cup won twice. After reverting to a player-coach role, he left to manage both Barrow and Workington before returning to St James' Park in 1962 for 13 seasons as manager, guiding his team back into the First Division and claiming United's first European trophy.

Gordon Lee
1975–77

Honours: League Cup runners-up 1975–76

Lee may have taken United to the League Cup Final in 1976, but is best remembered as the man who sold Malcolm Macdonald to Arsenal after falling out with the fans' favourite. When he left the club for Everton in January 1977, Newcastle sat in a highly creditable seventh place.

Richard Dinnis
1977

Honours: None

Deputy Dinnis carried on Lee's good work in his first season but managed to turn fifth place in 1976–77 into 22nd when he departed in November 1977.

Bill McGarry
1977–80
Honours: None

Relegation was an inevitability despite McGarry's efforts, but it was failure to lift them back into the top flight that eventually led to his departure in August 1980.

Arthur Cox
1980–84
Honours: None

Taking over in difficult times at Gallowgate, Cox slowly rebuilt the side, signing Kevin Keegan and leading the Magpies to promotion in fine style in 1984. With Newcastle fans anticipating further success the next season, he resigned to join Derby County, where he inspired a similar revival.

Jack Charlton
1984–85
Honours: None

Seemingly tailor-made for the United job, Charlton' s single season was not a happy one, 14th place in the League, early exits from the Cup competitions and the sale of Chris Waddle failing to endear him to the fans.

Willie McFaul
1985-88
Honours: None

Fairs Cup hero McFaul was in charge for just over three seasons, the best finish being eighth in 1987-88, but when he left in October 1988 United sat in a very precarious 19th position.

Jim Smith
1988-91
Honours: None

Smith was unable to stop United's descent into Division Two but took them into the promotion play-offs in 1989-90 where the ignominy of losing to Sunderland was too much for many supporters to take.

Ossie Ardiles
1991-92
Honours: None

Ex-Spurs favourite Ardiles did nothing to convince fans that better days lay ahead despite trying to encourage adventurous football. The team had lost all confidence and Division Three loomed by the time Sir John Hall recognised United's plight.

Kevin Keegan
1992–97
Honours: Division One Champions 1992–93

The second coming of Keegan heralded the change in fortunes St James' Park fans had been waiting for. Saving them from relegation to Division Three, he carried off the First Division Championship in 1992–93 and made third place in the Premiership a season later, completing an amazing turnaround. European football returned to Tyneside and, just as Keegan looked on the verge of taking a major honour, St James' Park resounded to another shock resignation.

Kenny Dalglish
1997–
Honours: None

Dalglish took over in January 1997 and led Keegan's team to second place in the Premier League and a European Cup berth. He had begun his managerial career at Liverpool in 1985 and amazingly achieved the League and FA Cup Double in his first year in charge, scoring the goal that clinched the title against Chelsea at Stamford Bridge.

Two years later Kenny's side strode to the title again with nine points to spare only to see their Double aspirations dashed by Wimbledon in the Cup Final. Even greater drama took place a year later when the Cup was won with local rivals Everton beaten at Wembley, only for Arsenal to deny Liverpool the title with a last-gasp goal.

It wasn't long though before Dalglish guided Liverpool to the title again, the trophy making its way back to Anfield a year later. It probably knew the way there by itself! However, Kenny shocked the football world as much as Keegan did when leaving Newcastle, when he quit Liverpool in 1991.

After a break from the game, Dalglish, now retired as a player, was tempted back into management by Blackburn. After leading them out of Division One via the play-offs he built a team which took the Premiership title to the small Lancashire town.

After stepping down from the manager's position at Ewood Park, Kenny stayed on as Director of Football and later accepted a position with Glasgow Rangers to assess potential signings – ironic, since he'd been a hero to the green half of Glasgow before moving to Merseyside. Dalglish won the first of his remarkable total of 39 major medals as a player back in 1972 when, at the age of 21, he helped Celtic to beat Hibs 6-1 in the Scottish Cup Final.

His plans for 1997-98 were hampered early on by injuries to Shearer and Asprilla, but it was his failure to spend money, having sold the likes of Ferdinand, Clark and Ginola, that caused concern. The jury is still out…

Best Season 2

In only the second season after the Second World War United were in determined mood: the previous campaign had seen them fall away after leading the Second Division promotion pack.

Bentley, Milburn, Shackleton and Wayman were still at the club, so firepower was not going to be too much of a problem, as was shown in the opening fixture, a 6-1 beating of Plymouth Argyle without Milburn in the line-up.

However, manager George Martin had very clear views as to the balance he required in his side and, by February, Bentley, Shackleton, Wayman and long-time favourite Tommy Pearson had left for pastures new. Incoming were wing-half Norman Dodgin and winger Willie McCall, both of whom would play important parts in the big push back into the top flight from which United had been absent since the end of season 1933-34.

As Christmas approached, United were up among the promotion hopefuls with only a couple of 3-0 defeats at Fulham and Plymouth to disturb the equilibrium. Milburn had got into a scoring groove, while Frank Brennan and Joe Harvey marshalled the defence with commanding authority, and enormous crowds were flocking to St James' Park for every game. But, as with all promotion bids, the crucial run-in from the new year onwards decided United's fate.

From the 3-1 home win on New Year's Day over West Bromwich Albion, only three reverses were suffered, all away from home. Interestingly, not one single away victory came United's way during this surge – indeed, only six wins came from their travels in total. The eventual success of the season was built on the 18 victories at St James' Park, visitors clearly overawed by the 50,000-plus crowds they had to face.

The crucial games came in April with two home fixtures against Fulham and Sheffield Wednesday, played within four days of each other. Both were duly won, the second game a truly epic encounter before nearly 66,500 paying customers: United had emergency winger Frank Houghton to thank for the two final goals in a 4–2 win which virtually guaranteed promotion. A 1–1 draw at Tottenham a week later confirmed a return to Division One as the Magpies finished in second place, three points behind champions Birmingham City – having secured two more wins and scored 17 more goals than the Midlanders.

1947-48 LEAGUE RECORD

Opponents	Home	Away
Barnsley	1-0	1-1
Birmingham City	1-0	0-0
Bradford Park Avenue	2-0	3-0
Brentford	1-0	0-1
Bury	1-0	5-3
Cardiff City	4-1	1-1
Chesterfield	2-3	1-0
Coventry City	0-0	1-1
Doncaster Rovers	2-0	3-0
Fulham	1-0	0-3
Leeds United	4-2	1-3
Leicester City	2-0	2-2
Luton Town	4-1	1-2
Millwall	1-0	1-2
Nottingham Forest	0-2	0-0
Plymouth Argyle	6-1	0-3
Sheffield Wednesday	4-2	0-1
Southampton	5-0	2-4
Tottenham Hotspur	1-0	1-1
West Bromwich Albion	3-1	1-0
West Ham United	1-0	2-0

The Grounds

Throughout its history Newcastle United FC has only ever played at St James' Park, a ground generally regarded as inhospitable by visiting teams.

United's previous incarnations were already using St James' Park (actually part of Leazes Park) before the club came into being in 1892. Descriptions of the ground at the time indicate that only one end had any kind of banking and only the Leazes Terrace could claim any kind of cover.

Although a small stand was subsequently built, things came to a head when promotion to the First Division was achieved in 1898. Apart from the lack of amenities for fans, the state of the pitch also gave cause for concern, its poor playing surface making it difficult to play good football. In 1899, work started in earnest to improve the situation: terracing appeared and a new structure, the Gallowgate Stand, sprung up, housing new dressing rooms. The pitch was relocated and the capacity grew to 30,000, that mark being hit for the first time against Sheffield United.

As the new century unfolded, a new lease was negotiated and further development took place. The West Stand took shape along Barrack Road and new terracing became a feature. The capacity shot up to over 52,000 and, on 6 September 1905, the new ground was officially opened before the 2-2 draw with Manchester City. Three years later a fire erupted in the new stand but little damage was done.

From 1905 until after the Second World War, few improvements were carried out, the exception being the covering of the Leazes enclosure. Various proposals made it onto the drawing board only to be thrown out by unsympathetic landlords or the council. In both World Wars the ground was taken over by the army, who left it each time in a state of disrepair.

Floodlights became a must in the 1950s, and in 1953 Celtic inaugurated Newcastle's illuminations, relatively unsophisticated lights which were replaced five years later by standard corner towers. In the same year, United's plan to build a large stand which would have increased capacity yet again fell foul of the authorities.

In the 1960s, the war between the council and Newcastle United really came to a head when St James' Park lost out as a World Cup venue because the ground didn't comply with the organisers' standards – which the club claimed it would have been only too happy to meet. There was even talk of United upping sticks and moving elsewhere.

In the next decade things at last started to move and a new East Stand took shape. The construction of the Leazes Stand seemed to be well under way when once again the authorities stepped in and called a halt due to its incompatibility with local houses. The problem was resolved...but not to the club's liking!

Since those confrontational days, club and council have slowly drawn closer together, the latter realising the prestige that a successful football club can bring to a city. Certainly, in past decades the Milburn Stand, built in the 1980s, would never have become reality – and, though a mid-1990s attempt to build a new, larger stadium on open ground failed to bear fruit, today's St James' Park is a home of which the supporters can feel proud.

Through The Years
July

1952
July
2

George Robledo scores seven goals in a game against Border in South Africa, an individual scoring record that's yet to be beaten by a United player.

1962
July
19

The birthdate of Paul Bracewell, a stalwart of Newcastle's midfield from 1992 to 1995. After leaving St James' for a third spell at Sunderland, he moved on to be part of Kevin Keegan's rebuilding process at Fulham – still going strong at 36.

1985
July
1

United receive £590,000 for the transfer of midfielder Chris Waddle to Tottenham. His departure robs the team of a major talent, and he will go on to be sold for over £1 million to Marseille in 1989.

1988
July
6

In a carbon copy of the Waddle move, the awesomely talented Paul Gascoigne leaves United for White Hart Lane. This time, at least, the London club has to shell out a British transfer record sum of £2.3 million.

1996
July
29

In a welcome reversal of previous summers, Newcastle's team is augmented and not depleted. The services of Geordie-born striker Alan Shearer are secured when Kevin Keegan pays Blackburn Rovers a world record fee of £15 million.

Attendances

As with most successful clubs, Newcastle's most impressive attendances come from an era when ground capacities were much greater than in the post-Taylor Report decade, when safety became paramount.

What club wouldn't like to boast an average home turn-out of 56,299 as United could in the 1947–48 season? Astoundingly they were then in Division Two, and followed that figure with a 53,702 average in 1948–49. United, in fact, topped the national home attendance averages for the first three seasons after World War II.

In many respects, the May 1951 gate of 60,000 for a reserve-team fixture against Leeds United stands out as one of the most remarkable attendances of all time – the reason behind it being exhibition to the fans of the recently-won FA Cup. It should be noted that United's reserves were no strangers to good support, averaging close to 17,000 for home games in the 1933–34 season.

Many of the outstanding St James' Park crowds have come against Sunderland, exceeding 55,000 on a number of occasions, and in 1901 it is estimated that close to 70,000 attempted to gain access when the capacity was only 30,000. Trouble ensued and the game was abandoned before kick-off.

The all-time record gate remains 68,368 for the visit of Chelsea on 3 September 1930, thanks to the return of Hughie Gallagher who had been transferred to the London club in the close season. Countless supporters found viewing points both on top of the stand and in the trees outside the ground.

United fans are noted for their passionate commitment to the club. For instance, 47,124 devotees turned up for the friendly with Sweden's IFK Norrkoping in the 1946-47 season, while nearly 45,000 watched another friendly, this time with Liverpool, a year later. This immediate postwar period was a boom time for attendances in general, when the footballing public were desperate for a return to normality and top-class soccer. Wartime crowds were often impressive too, 54,954 being registered for a League fixture with Manchester City and 52,836 for a Cup game against Sheffield United during the Second World War.

With such a devoted following, it's difficult to believe that attendances slumped to a postwar low of 17,350 in 1980-81, producing an aggregate light-years adrift from the record 1,186,424 who'd crammed into St James' Park in 1946-47.

European competition brought crowds approaching 60,000, including the 59,234 who witnessed the first leg of the Inter Cities Fairs Cup Final versus Hungary's Ujpest Dozsa in 1969. Testimonial matches are also habitually well attended, over 40,000 being welcomed to both Jackie Milburn and Bobby Mitchell's fund-raisers in the 1960s.

Away from home, United have attracted even larger attendances, the 70,787 who packed into Maine Road in December 1948 for a Manchester United fixture (Old Trafford was closed due to bomb damage) represents their highest figure for a League match. 70,000-plus figures have also been recorded for League games at Tottenham and Chelsea, while over 75,000 assembled at Ibrox Park for an Inter-Cities Fairs Cup fixture in United's winning season.

All the Wembley Cup Final wins were in front of 100,000, as was the 1976 League Cup Final where United finished runners-up, but for the largest crowd the club has ever played before we must look back to the 1905 FA Cup Final at Crystal Palace. United and Aston Villa attracted 101,117 to a game the Midlanders won 2-0.

DREAM TEAM 2

With only one win in the first dozen League games, an air of gloom hung over Tyneside and fans were looking forward to a desperate time of survival. But the class of 1968-69 will forever be remembered for bringing the first European trophy to St James' Park.

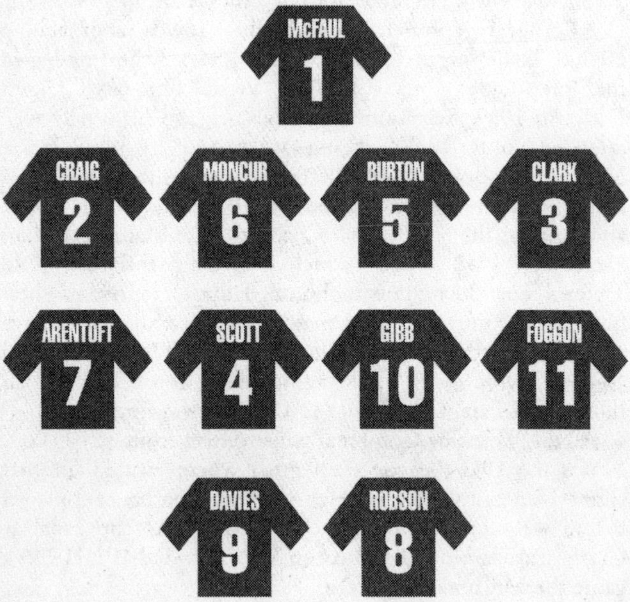

Goalkeeper **Willie McFaul**
Played in every competitive game that season, his consistent keeping going a long way towards United carrying off the trophy.

Right-back **David Craig**
Regarded as one of the best backs in the home countries, Craig's injury jinx took over again in 1968-69 but he did not miss that two-legged Final. Played in over 400 games for the Magpies.

Left-back **Frank Clark**
A great servant over 12 seasons, Clark's experience and level head proved invaluable when the going got tough.

Central defender **Bobby Moncur**
Captain who lead by example and contributed those vital goals. No captain has deserved to lift a trophy more.

Central defender **Ollie Burton**

A versatile customer, Burton operated with Moncur in the middle of the defence. Like Craig, prone to injury throughout his career.

Midfielder **Jimmy Scott**

In and out of the team but scored four priceless goals in Europe. Eventually moved on to Crystal Palace in 1970.

Midfielder **Benny Arentoft**

Dane Arentoft came into the side as things were coming to the boil and settled in comfortably between Scott and Gibb. Scored in the second leg of the Fairs Cup Final.

Midfielder **Tommy Gibb**

A player who liked to go at opposition defences, who also had a high workrate. Not always appreciated by the fans, but good enough to rack up over 230 games in the black and white stripes.

Forward **Bryan Robson**

A natural-born finisher who was unlucky in not being allowed to display his predatory instincts at international level.

Forward **Wyn Davies**

In many respects a throwback to a previous era, a great target man whose ball-winning in the air laid on chances for his colleagues and caused havoc in opponents' defences. On retiring, he had taken part in close to 700 games, having represented a whole host of clubs.

Forward **Alan Foggon**

Made an explosive entry into the Fairs Cup Final by coming off the bench and scoring the winning goal in the second leg. Moved to Cardiff City in 1971, taking his treasured memory with him.

NUFC Trivia Quiz

Can you fathom these 40 testing questions on Newcastle past and present?
Answers on page 190-191.

1 Who was the goalkeeper when United won the Inter-Cities Fairs Cup?

2 For whom did Faustino Asprilla play prior to joining the Magpies?

3 With which League club did Peter Beardsley start his League career?

4 Against whom did Kevin Keegan make his St James' Park debut in August 1982?

5 Which player signed for United from Paris St Germain?

6 Which team put United out of the 1996-97 FA Cup?

7 Newcastle scored seven goals against which First Division opponents in 1996-97?

8 Which international competition did the Magpies win in 1972-73?

9 When playing at Celtic which nickname did Roy Aitken acquire? Was it (a) the Bear (b) the Gorilla or (c) the Tiger?

10 Andy Cole started his career as a trainee with which club?

11 Was Steve Howey born in (a) Newcastle (b) Sunderland or (c) Gateshead?

12 Malcolm Macdonald played for two League clubs before United: can you name them?

13 To whom did United lose in the Final of the 1976 League Cup?

14 In which Division Two League position did the Magpies finish in 1983-84?

15 Which ex-St James' Park favourite managed Sunderland to FA Cup victory in 1973?

16 For which Scottish club did Hughie Gallagher play before signing for United?

17 Who scored in every round of the 1951 successful Cup run?

18 Which forward scored two successive hat-tricks in the 1950-51 season?

19 For which Irish League club did George Eastham play?

20 To which club did Wyn Davies move in 1971?

21 Which future England captain wore the Number 8 shirt for United for four games in 1982?

22 Who followed Malcolm Macdonald to Arsenal in 1976?

23 Who captained United to FA Cup Victory in 1955?

24 United were beaten by whom in the 1974 FA Cup Final?

25 Imre Varadi left St James' Park for which club?

26 Which ex-Newcastle star won a European Cup winner's medal in 1967?

27 Alf McMichael made 431 League and Cup appearances for United – but how many goals did he score?

28 Who joined United in October 1982 from Tulsa Roughnecks?

29 Who was the only forward not to score in the 13-0 thrashing of Newport County in 1946: Milburn, Bentley, Wayman, Shackleton or Pearson?

30 Which Newcastle player scored four goals in an international against Northern Ireland in 1929?

31 From which country did Preben 'Benny' Arentoft come?

32 How many League goals did Alan Shearer score in Blackburn colours? Was it (a) 153 (b) 112 or (c) 129?

33 In which year did Paul Bracewell sign from Sunderland?

34 How many goals did Kevin Keegan score against Rotherham in October 1982?

35 Who was United's first £100,000 signing?

36 Who scored four goals on his debut versus Leeds United in 1989?

37 In the 1970s who managed the Magpies for only 36 games?

38 Who knocked United out of the 1969-70 European Fairs Cup?

39 Jackie Milburn moved to which club as player-manager in 1957?

40 Which player made his debut in February 1994 after signing from Norwich?

Through The Years
August

1926
August
28

The opening League game in what would be a Championship-winning season turned into the Hughie Gallagher show as the skilful Scot scored all of United's goals in a 4-0 dismissal of Aston Villa.

1971
August
21

Malcolm Macdonald snatched a hat-trick in his first home game, as the Magpies beat Liverpool 3-2. The same month had seen Kenny Hibbitt, one of Supermac's main midfield providers, signed from Leeds United for a bargain fee of £30,000.

1978
August

Long-serving full-back David Craig signed as an apprentice. The future Northern Ireland international would make the first of over 400 appearances three years later.

1982
August
28

Newly-signed Kevin Keegan scored the only goal of the opening League game as United defeated Queens Park Rangers before a crowd of over 35,000 at St James' Park. (The last home game of 1981-82 had been watched by under 10,000 people.) Fans were queuing for the game from the early hours of the morning and, when he eventually arrived on the pitch, he received a tumultuous reception. The Messiah had arrived!

1985
August
17

United started their second season back in the top flight in fine style with Peter Beardsley on song and the exciting young talent of Paul Gascoigne being unveiled to the fans. Five games unbeaten looked like the perfect opening, but the Magpies were destined to finish in only 11th position.

1989
August
19

Signed during the close season from Portsmouth, striker Mick Quinn made a spectacular debut against Leeds United, scoring four goals in a 5-2 win. This started a sequence of nine goals in five games for the likeable Liverpudlian.

TRANSFERS

Transfer fees have come a long way since the turn of the century, passing from the few hundred pounds to the low to high thousands and on to multi-million deals in an indecently short space of time.

The terms of players' contracts also altered as the century progressed, most significantly with the abolition of the minimum wage, the altering of the 'retain and transfer' system fought over by United's George Eastham and, most recently, the Bosman ruling of September 1995 which allows players their freedom at the end of a contract. Kevin Keegan decries the Bosman ruling in his autobiography, claiming it 'took the guts out of running a football club' but both Keegan (now at Fulham) and United are likely to profit from this legislation at some time in the future.

Keegan had no chance of benefiting from this ruling when he had to break the world record to sign Alan Shearer from Blackburn for £15 million in July 1996 – a seemingly astronomical fee, albeit for a proven performer. Only the previous year Manchester United had paid the Magpies a record £7 million (£6 million plus Keith Gillespie) for the signature of Andy Cole, a fee that seemed highly inflated until Cole finally started to rack up the goals in 1997-98.

The above figures are a far cry from the £400 the Magpies paid Aston Villa in February 1903 for RB Templeton – a player who only stayed until November the following year before moving on to Arsenal for £375. It wasn't a great financial deal, but at least the directors had a profit to show years later when they felt they had to sell Hughie Gallagher. The purchase price in 1925 was £6,500, while five years later Chelsea paid United £10,000 for the privilege of taking him south.

Similarly, profits have been turned on other players such as Len Shackleton, bought in 1946 for £13,000 and sold in 1948 for £20,050, and Malcolm Macdonald, who arrived in 1971 costing £180,000 and left five years later for £333,333. Yet who could put a price on the fans' dismay?

Less astute dealing took place in 1988 when a total of £3.25 million was spent on five players – Dave Beasant, Kenny Sansom, Andy Thorn, John Robertson and John Hendrie – who failed to save the Magpies from relegation to Division Two at the end of the 1988-89 season. Only a few years earlier, Arthur Cox had assembled his promotion team by spending wisely, £100,000 on both McDermott and Keegan, £75,000 for McCreery and £120,000 on Beardsley being perfect examples.

Beardsley was transferred to Liverpool in 1987 for a record fee of £1.9 million, a figure topped a year later when Tottenham captured Paul Gascoigne for £2.3 million. Chris Waddle joined Spurs in 1985, the £590,000 paid comparing well with the £1,000 the Magpies had paid in 1980.

With Sir John Hall's millions at his disposal, Kevin Keegan spent big after reaching the top flight. £6 million secured Les Ferdinand from QPR in June 1995, only 15 months after £2.7 million Darren Peacock arrived from the same club. Anderlecht pocketed £2.5 million for Philippe Albert, while Paris SG were probably delighted with the similar fee they received for David Ginola. The £2 million lavished on Ruel Fox bought a typical crowd pleaser while eyebrows were raised at Warren Barton's £4 million price tag, but the £1.75 million Andy Cole deal will stand as Keegan's 'best buy'.

Kenny Dalglish has money to spend, but his moves into the transfer market have yet to prove fruitful.

Worst Season 2

Having finished in fifth position in 1976-77 despite the upheaval produced by the departure of manager Gordon Lee, Richard Dinnis's side had established themselves as one of the leading clubs in the top flight.

Few could have envisaged the disastrous season the Magpies were about to embark upon when Leeds United were defeated 3-2 in the opening game, thanks to two goals from Micky Burns and one from Alan Kennedy.

That victory would be the last in the League until a single 22 October win broke a run of ten successive League defeats in which only eight goals were scored. To add insult to injury, Millwall dumped United out of the League Cup, the only solace coming from a 4-0 win over Bohemians in the UEFA Cup.

Dinnis's inevitable departure in November heralded the arrival of experienced ex-Wolves chief Bill McGarry to tackle the thankless task of avoiding relegation. Exit from the UEFA Cup did nothing for club confidence, but three straight wins in December without conceding a goal lifted United's fans. This was a false dawn, however, for the club was about to enter one of its worst periods with only one more League win before season's end. The FA Cup bought little comfort for the suffering faithful, a 4-1 February defeat by Wrexham adding to already substantial woes.

Apart from Dinnis, two other major figures left St James' Park as the Magpies sank towards (the then) Division Two. Tommy Craig left for Aston Villa in January and Alan

Gowling, whose most successful period for the club had come two seasons earlier, headed for Bolton in March. Micky Burns, the club's leading scorer that season, would depart in August to take up the post of player-coach at Cardiff City, the exodus being completed by Alan Kennedy who joined Liverpool that same month.

So United slid down the ladder to Division Two, having virtually hoisted the white flag from the beginning of September when they sat in 20th place. They never improved on that position, recording only six League victories and losing 26 times. All but the most loyal of fans started to vote with their feet, the opening day's 36,700 having dwindled to a paltry 7,986 souls by the final home game against Norwich. Clearly, matters had reached an all-time low.

1977-78 LEAGUE RECORD

Opponents	Home	Away
Arsenal	1-2	1-1
Aston Villa	1-1	0-2
Birmingham City	1-1	0-3
Bristol City	1-1	1-3
Chelsea	1-0	2-2
Coventry City	1-2	0-0
Derby County	1-2	1-1
Everton	0-2	4-4
Ipswich Town	0-1	1-2
Leeds United	3-2	2-0
Leicester City	2-0	0-3
Liverpool	0-2	0-2
Manchester City	2-2	0-4
Manchester United	2-2	2-3
Middlesbrough	2-4	0-2
Norwich City	2-2	1-2
Nottingham Forest	0-2	0-2
Queens Park Rangers	0-3	1-0
West Bromwich Albion	0-3	0-2
West Ham United	2-3	0-1
Wolverhampton Wanderers	4-0	0-1

The Magpies A-Z

For fascinating facts, there's no beating this Newcastle United alphabet!

A could stand for any number of distinguished United players, but the name of Bill Appleyard is a deserving one as he scored 87 goals in 145 appearances between 1902 and 1908.

B is represented by the Bells, six players of that surname having worn the black and white stripes.

C stands for the Crystal Palace, a graveyard of a venue for United at the start of the century. Between 1905 and 1911, the Magpies contested five FA Cup Finals on that ground, losing four times and drawing once.

D can only mean Kenny Dalglish, who very quickly learnt what a difficult act Kevin Keegan was to follow and, as the 1997-98 season unfolded, found himself under increasing scrutiny.

E means Elswick Rugby Club, where the first Tyneside organised football match is said to have been played in 1877, although reports indicate that 'organised' might have been an inappropriate word.

F could stand for the fortune Sir John Hall has pumped into United, placing them among the elite of the game but so far failing to secure the major trophy Tyneside so desperately wants to claim.

G is for Tony Green whose flame burnt ever so briefly at St James' Park before serious injury curtailed his career in 1973 at the age of only 27. His stylish but fleeting contribution to the United cause is remembered fondly by fans.

H is represented by Percy Harper, the referee who happily awarded the equalising goal in the famous 'over the line' FA Cup Final of 1932 and Mick Harford, a Magpie for a matter of minutes in 1982. His transfer was an expedient measure to resolve a financial matter involving Bristol City.

I belongs to Jim Iley, who captained United to promotion in 1965. In seven years he made nearly 250 appearances before moving on to become player-manager with Peterborough United. He retired as a player with over 600 games to his credit.

J means the Japan Cup, which was won in 1983.

K only stands for Kevin Keegan (if you don't count Alan Kennedy, Dick Keith, Vic Keeble, Matt Kingsley *et al*) who helped revitalise the fortunes of United as both player and manager.

L constitutes a low point – Wilf Low, to be exact. The Scottish international won an FA Cup winner's medal in 1910, one of over 370 appearances he made in United colours. After retirement, he moved to the administrative staff until his untimely death in a road accident in 1933.

M is taken care of by Jackie Milburn, who still sits on a pinnacle as far as older supporters are concerned.

N is for Newcastle Rangers who took part in the inaugural game at St James' Park, or West End and East End who both played there and were forerunners of the present club.

O is for Ostrava, the birthplace of Pavel Srnicek, and Ronald Orr, the Scot who graced St James' between 1901-08.

P means the pleasure many in the game have derived from watching United in the 1990s, their emphasis on attack refreshing in a game littered with 'safety first' sides.

Q stands for two Quinns: C Quinn, the winger who played in United's first ever League season and Mick Quinn, whose 34 goals contributed greatly to making the play-offs in 1989.

R is for relegation, which United have experienced on numerous occasions.

S simply stands for Smith – Jack Smith, a signing from

Huddersfield in 1934 with an outstanding strike rate of 73 goals in 112 games in the 1930s. He left Tyneside for Old Trafford in 1938 amid much protest.

T is for trial matches, for many years held before the start of each season and involving first team versus reserves. Often well attended, these disappeared in the 1950s.

U stands for the uproar caused by the shock resignations of managers like Gordon Lee and Kevin Keegan and the universal joy shown when signing Alan Shearer.

V stands for victory in six FA Cup Finals and four Championships. It could equally stand for the vast army of supporters who would dearly like those figures added to!

W brings us to George Weah, whom Keegan thought he had signed in 1995 from Paris St Germain. Keegan did not get his man and Weah ended up with AC Milan.

X marks the spot where Geordie fans believe God told them to pay homage – St James' Park!

Y is for 'yawn', implied by some about the goalless 1911 FA Cup Final. United lost the replay to Bradford City, 1-0.

Z stands for zebra, the animal the Geordies just might have been likened to if the Magpie hadn't got there first.

The Reign Of King Kevin

Five years that changed the face of football on Tyneside – the man and his legacy.

When former player Kevin Keegan returned to St James' Park on 5 February 1992 in what the press dubbed 'The Second Coming', Newcastle United FC was in freefall. His surprise resignation as manager in January 1997, nearly five years later, came at a point when the club had once again become a force in English football. St James's Park was full for every match, and the club was on its way to a second consecutive runner's-up slot in the Premiership – just one step away from the top rung of the footballing ladder they'd last occupied in 1927.

The situation Keegan inherited from Ossie Ardiles could be traced back to 1990 when, after finishing third, they'd bowed out in the play-offs to Sunderland. Their bitter rivals had ended the season three places lower but went on to be promoted. The following season saw Newcastle slump to 11th and manager Jim Smith gave way to former Spurs and Argentina star Ossie Ardiles, more recently Swindon player-manager.

Keegan had been out of the game, through choice, since being airlifted from St James's Park in triumph in 1984, when promotion was achieved in his second season on Tyneside. 'I will kick the last competitive ball of my career in a Newcastle shirt,' he'd said. Now he was back, he needed an assistant on whom he could rely, and looked no further than Terry

McDermott, the man who'd played alongside him in that successful Magpies team and who, like him, had been a Liverpool superstar in the 1970s. The combination of Keegan's inspiration and 'Terry Mac's perspiration was an effective one.

When Keegan and his trusted lieutenant arrived, the club was 23rd in the Second Division and leaking goals by the netful. He immediately stiffened the defence with battle-hardened 29-year-old centre-half Brian Kilcline, adding another seasoned campaigner to midfield in ex-Everton and Eire midfielder Kevin Sheedy, and bringing back striker Mick Quinn from the reserves. Quinn responded to the faith shown in him with goals.

The crowds too responded to the return of the messiah. The visit of Charlton Athletic for the last home game before his arrival attracted 15,663 fans – a game lost 4-3. The 3-0 win against Bristol City three days after Keegan's arrival drew a healthy 29,263. Sir John Hall, the man behind Newcastle's ambitions, was being paid back already.

A win against Jim Smith's Portsmouth in the penultimate game was secured with a goal from Eire international David Kelly, but Newcastle still weren't out of the woods. It took an own goal by Leicester's Mike Walsh in the last game of the season to push them to a safe 20th place and condemn Plymouth, Brighton and Port Vale to the drop.

With English football in the throes of a revolution, the top flight – now renamed the Premiership – was more than ever the place to be. Keegan bought big – and started at the back with full-backs John Beresford (Portsmouth) and Barry Venison (Liverpool). Other buys would include Charlton's inspirational midfielder Rob Lee,

Leeds' wide-man Scott Sellars and Czech keeper Pavel Srnicek, who took over from Tommy Wright and proved more than worth his place.

But his biggest coup was the capture in March 1993 of Andy Cole, a goalpoacher who contributed 12 goals in 12 games, as Newcastle brought the Championship trophy to St James' Park. It was no surprise – the first 11 matches had all been won, giving the Magpies a third of their eventual total of 96 points in just a quarter of the games available. A last-game 7-1 win over Leicester hinted the top flight would reverberate to the Toon Army's battle cry – and the first Premiership season would exceed all expectations by ending in European qualification.

Keegan had reshaped his squad with the next five years in mind, but went back to the future for 31-year-old Peter Beardsley, his team-mate in the glory years of the 1980s, whose return to Tyneside saw him recalled to Terry Venables' England team.

Darren Peacock had come from QPR on 1994's transfer deadline day for a club record £2.7 million and was joined by Belgian Philippe Albert and Swiss Marc Hottiger. Only two of the first eight games were won, but Cole and Beardsley sparked in the same way Keegan and Beardsley had a decade earlier and 55 League goals resulted in a third-place finish.

Despite another great foundation with a six-game, 22-goal maximum start, the 1994-95 season was, perhaps inevitably, an anti-climax after such an amazing return to the top flight. Lee, Venison and Cole were all struck with injuries and a UEFA Cup campaign that started with a 10-2 win against Royal Antwerp ended at the next hurdle against Bilbao. The Magpies finished sixth, just outside the UEFA Cup qualification zone, a slump having followed FA Cup defeat by eventual winners Everton.

Keegan had risked everything by selling star striker Andy Cole and waiting until summer to replace him with QPR and England's Les Ferdinand. At the same time he invested in French wide player David Ginola from Paris St Germain to supply the ammunition alongside Keith Gillespie, a Northern Ireland international winger who arrived as £1 million makeweight in the Cole deal.

Defence was rebuilt from the back. Goalkeeper Shaka Hislop came from Reading, while England full-back Warren Barton came from Wimbledon. This new rearguard proved its efficiency by only losing once in the League by the end of November. Then Keegan repeated his tactic of buying when the team was strong, Colombian marksman Faustino Asprilla being added to the squad in a £7.5 million deal. But while Cole had found a hot streak, 'Tino' proved less of a hit: Beardsley was pushed wide to accommodate him, and the balance of the side was fatally altered.

Manchester United's single-goal win at St James's in early March loosened Newcastle's grip on the title, and a 4-3 defeat at Anfield in April, the lead changing hands three times, sounded the death knell on the Magpies' Championship chances. Never mind, but it was the best showing since the 1920s, the disappointment was palpable.

Yet despair turned to elation when Geordie-born England striker Alan Shearer 'came home' from Blackburn to play alongside Les Ferdinand – the fee a national record £15 million. Another ex-Blackburn international David Batty added bite to the midfield, and when Manchester United were vanquished 5-0 in October, it seemed a second Championship challenge was on.

But a poor run between then and the last game of 1996 when Spurs were demolished 7-1 said otherwise, and with the forthcoming flotation of the club on the stock exchange adding even more pressure, 'King Kev' announced his abdication in early January. 'I feel I have taken the club as far as I can,' he said, 'and that it would be in the best interests of all concerned if I resigned.'

Kenny Dalglish, the man who, ironically, had replaced Keegan when he left Liverpool for Europe in 1977, was the chosen successor, and having won the title with two different clubs was clearly an appropriate selection. He duly led Newcastle to second place, pipping Arsenal in the last game of the season and securing a berth in the following year's European Cup (this being the first time the English runners-up were admitted).

Keegan returned to the game in the autumn of 1997 as chief operating officer at Fulham, enticed back to football by the millions of Mohamed El Fayed and the prospect of awakening a sleeping giant.

Whatever he achieved by the banks of the Thames, however, would pale in comparison with the turnaround in fortunes he'd overseen on Tyneside from 1992.

Kevin Keegan presided over 249 games as Newcastle boss in just under five years. Of these, 138 (55.4 per cent) were won, 50 (20.1 per cent) were drawn and 61 (24.5 per cent) lost.

St James's Park fans were rewarded for their attendance by a 71 per cent victory rate, while the travelling faithful had a four out of ten chance of seeing the Magpies come away with all three points.

Even after just half a season in charge, attendances at St James' were up from an average of 16,834 to 21,148 – an increase of some 25 per cent. The season of his departure saw crowds averaging 36,466, all paying Premiership prices.

THROUGH THE YEARS SEPTEMBER

1895
September
6

Newcastle United Football Club Company Limited. was formed out of its predecessor the East End club whose officials felt the need for change due to lack of support and, consequently, income.

1898
September
3

The Magpies played their first ever Division One fixture, at home to Wolverhampton Wanderers, losing 4-2. This heralded a disastrous start to the season: not until 5 November did they record their first win – at the eleventh attempt!

1962
September

Midfield maestro Jim Iley arrived at St James' Park from Nottingham Forest. Iley distinguished himself in nearly 250 games, often in the role of captain.

1968
September
11

United played their first ever game in European competition, defeating Dutch giants Feyenoord 4-0. Davies, Gibb, Bryan Robson and Scott were the scorers.

1979
September

During a run of four League wins, Alan Shoulder scored four penalties in three games. Out of a total goal tally of 21 for the season, nine came from the spot.

1992
September
12

Despite winning their opening five League matches during Kevin Keegan's promotion season as manager, United only went top of the (old) Second Division after today's 3-1 victory against Portsmouth and stayed there until the end of the season. Good times were returning to Tyneside at last!

Bogey Teams

All top-flight teams have opposition they would prefer to avoid due to a history of bad results – or simply because the club in question plays in a style that disrupts the most carefully-honed system.

Teams from the lower divisions often turn into giant-killers when drawn against superior opposition in the FA Cup, and Newcastle have fallen victim to lowly opposition on more than one occasion.

Probably the most famous blip in United's Cup history concerns Hereford United who, as they are now, were a non-League club in 1972. Hereford had forced a draw at St James' Park two weeks earlier, a feat in itself, but completed the job in front of their own supporters by winning 2-1 thanks to a rocket shot from Ronnie Radford.

The goal haunts Magpie supporters even today, as it was captured by BBC cameras (a young John Motson commentating) and is regularly replayed whenever the subject of FA Cup shocks gets an airing.

Other non-League sides which have also accounted for United in the FA Cup include Southampton St Mary's (twice, in 1898 and 1900), Crystal Palace in 1907 and more recently Bedford Town in 1964. The latter result was perhaps not so much of a shock, as the 1960s saw United fail at the first hurdle four times. If such a thing as a bogey ground exists, the Geordies must have felt that Crystal Palace fitted the bill, for they lost their first three Finals there in the early part of the century.

United's problem team in the Cup, post-Second World War, was Charlton Athletic, who inflicted successive defeats on Milburn and company in 1946-47 and 1947-48. The most painful of the two reverses was a 4-0 Semi-Final drubbing at Elland Road.

In the 1980s United surpassed their sad FA Cup record of the 1960s, being eliminated in the Third Round five times, and in 1987-88 Wimbledon put them out of both domestic Cup competitions. United could not beat them in the League that season either.

Like all clubs United have gone through poor periods against certain opponents despite above-average performances against others. Chelsea seemed to have a hoodoo on the Magpies from the mid 1950s to the early 1960s. The Londoners were unbeaten in a sequence of 15 games and, in season 1958-59, beat United no less than three times – 6-5 and 2-1 in the League and 4-1 in the Cup.

Before the turn of the century, Burton Swifts' ground proved a real graveyard for the Magpies with five consecutive losses recorded up to promotion in 1897-98. The games between the two clubs were generally high-scoring affairs with United likely to score a hatful at home and concede just as many in the away fixture. The Swifts were bidden a none too tearful goodbye when Division One status was achieved.

Both Manchester clubs proved to be a thorn in United's side during the mid 1970s. City's 5-1 win in 1975 started the rot, while the following year saw them meet and lose to the same opposition in the Final of the League Cup to complete a season in which they lost twice to United.

Things got worse in 1976-77, with failure to record a victory over either team in the League, topped by an exit to United 7-2 in the League Cup and a 3-1 reversal to City in the FA Cup. Predictably, when relegated in 1978, the preceding season had witnessed no triumphs over either the Reds or Light Blues.

League Record

The century started brightly on the League ladder – can the Magpies end it as successfully?

Season	Division	P	W	D	L	F-A	Pts	Pos
1893-94	Two	28	15	6	7	66-39	36	4th
1894-95	Two	30	12	3	15	72-84	27	10th
1895-96	Two	30	16	2	12	73-50	34	5th
1896-97	Two	30	17	1	12	56-52	35	5th
1897-98	Two	30	21	3	6	64-32	45	2nd
● Division Two Runners-up ●								
1898-99	One	34	11	8	15	49-48	30	13th
1899-1900	One	34	13	10	11	53-43	36	5th
1900-01	One	34	14	10	10	42-37	38	6th
1901-02	One	34	14	9	11	48-34	37	3rd
1902-03	One	34	14	4	16	41-51	32	14th
1903-04	One	34	18	6	10	58-45	42	4th
1904-05	One	34	23	2	9	72-33	48	1st
★ Division One Champions ★								
1905-06	One	38	18	7	13	74-48	43	4th
1906-07	One	38	22	7	9	74-46	51	1st
★ Division One Champions ★								
1907-08	One	38	15	12	11	65-54	42	4th
1908-09	One	38	24	5	9	65-41	53	1st
★ Division One Champions ★								

Season	Division	P	W	D	L	F-A	Pts	Pos
1909-10	One	38	19	7	12	70-56	45	4th
1910-11	One	38	15	10	13	61-43	40	8th
1911-12	One	38	18	8	12	64-50	44	3rd
1912-13	One	38	13	8	17	47-47	34	14th
1913-14	One	38	13	11	14	39-48	37	11th
1914-15	One	38	11	10	17	46-48	32	15th
1919-20	One	42	17	9	16	44-39	43	8th
1920-21	One	42	20	10	12	66-45	50	5th
1921-22	One	42	18	10	14	59-45	46	7th
1922-23	One	42	18	12	12	45-37	48	4th
1923-24	One	42	17	10	15	60-54	44	9th
1924-25	One	42	16	16	10	61-42	48	6th
1925-26	One	42	16	10	16	84-75	42	10th
1926-27	One	42	25	6	11	96-58	56	1st
★ Division One Champions ★								
1927-28	One	42	15	13	14	79-81	43	9th
1928-29	One	42	19	6	17	70-72	44	10th
1929-30	One	42	15	7	20	71-92	37	19th
1930-31	One	42	15	6	21	78-87	36	17th
1931-32	One	42	18	6	18	80-87	42	11th
1932-33	One	42	22	5	15	71-63	49	5th
1933-34	One	42	10	14	18	68-77	34	21st
Relegated								
1934-35	Two	42	22	4	16	89-68	48	6th
1935-36	Two	42	20	6	16	88-79	46	8th
1936-37	Two	42	22	5	15	80-56	49	4th
1937-38	Two	42	14	8	20	51-58	36	19th
1938-39	Two	42	18	10	14	61-48	46	9th
1946-47	Two	42	19	10	13	95-62	48	5th
1947-48	Two	42	24	8	10	72-41	56	2nd
● Division Two Runners-up ●								

Season	Division	P	W	D	L	F-A	Pts	Pos
1948-49	One	42	20	12	10	70-56	52	4th
1949-50	One	42	19	12	11	77-55	50	5th
1950-51	One	42	18	13	11	62-53	49	4th
1951-52	One	42	18	9	15	98-73	45	8th
1952-53	One	42	14	9	19	59-70	37	16th
1953-54	One	42	14	10	18	72-77	38	15th
1954-55	One	42	17	9	16	89-77	43	8th
1955-56	One	42	17	7	18	85-70	41	11th
1956-57	One	42	14	8	20	67-87	36	17th
1957-58	One	42	12	8	22	73-81	32	19th
1958-59	One	42	17	7	18	80-80	41	11th
1959-60	One	42	18	8	16	82-78	44	8th
1960-61	One	42	11	10	21	86-109	32	21st
Relegated								
1961-62	Two	42	15	9	18	64-58	39	11th
1962-63	Two	42	18	11	13	79-59	47	7th
1963-64	Two	42	20	5	17	74-69	45	8th
1964-65	Two	42	24	9	9	81-45	57	1st
★ **Division Two Champions** ★								
1965-66	One	42	14	9	19	50-63	37	15th
1966-67	One	42	12	9	21	39-81	33	20th
1967-68	One	42	13	15	14	54-67	41	10th
1968-69	One	42	15	14	13	61-55	44	9th
1969-70	One	42	17	13	12	57-35	47	7th
1970-71	One	42	14	13	15	44-46	41	12th
1971-72	One	42	15	11	16	49-52	41	11th
1972-73	One	42	16	13	13	60-51	45	9th
1973-74	One	42	13	12	17	49-48	38	15th
1974-75	One	42	15	9	18	59-72	39	15th
1975-76	One	42	15	9	18	71-62	39	15th
1976-77	One	42	18	13	11	64-49	49	5th

Season	Division	P	W	D	L	F-A	Pts	Pos
1977-78	One	42	6	10	26	42-78	22	21st
Relegated								
1978-79	Two	42	17	8	17	51-55	42	8th
1979-80	Two	42	15	14	13	53-49	44	9th
1980-81	Two	42	14	14	14	30-45	42	11th
1981-82	Two	42	18	8	16	52-50	62	9th
1982-83	Two	42	18	13	11	75-53	67	5th
1983-84	Two	42	24	8	10	85-53	80	3rd
Promoted								
1984-85	One	42	13	13	16	55-70	52	14th
1985-86	One	42	17	12	13	67-72	63	11th
1986-87	One	42	12	11	19	47-65	47	17th
1987-88	One	40	14	14	12	55-53	56	8th
1988-89	One	38	7	10	21	32-63	31	20th
Relegated								
1989-90	Two	46	22	14	10	80-55	80	3rd
1990-91	Two	46	14	17	15	49-56	59	11th
1991-92	Two	46	13	13	20	66-84	52	20th
1992-93	One	46	29	9	8	92-38	96	1st
Division One Champions								
1993-94	Premier	42	23	8	11	82-41	77	3rd
1994-95	Premier	42	20	12	10	67-47	72	6th
1995-96	Premier	38	24	6	8	66-37	78	2nd
Premiership Runners-up								
1996-97	Premier	38	19	11	8	73-40	68	2nd
Premiership Runners-up								

Through The Years
October

1901
October

In a season when United finished third in Division One, Notts County were beaten at both ends of the month, the second time 8-0 at St James' Park. Regular scorers Ronald Orr and Jock Peddie, with four and three goals respectively, helped run up what was at the time United's record victory.

1946
October
5

Bobby Cowell joined in 1943 but had to wait until today to make his League debut in the 13-0 defeat of Newport. Cowell won three Cup winner's medals in United's colours.

1958
October
11

Welsh International Ivor Allchurch made an immediate impact after signing from Swansea, scoring twice on his debut in a 3-1 victory over Leicester City. Allchurch finished the season having totalled 16 goals in 26 appearances.

1962
October

Full-back Frank Clark began his marathon stay at St James' Park – a spell which would see him appear in over 450 League and Cup games.

1966
October

United paid out a record club fee of £80,000 for Bolton's Welsh international striker Wyn Davies.

1996
October
20

Reigning Premiership Champions Manchester United were beaten 5-0 at St James' Park with goals from Peacock, Ginola, Ferdinand, Shearer and Albert. Also this month, Newcastle beat the once-proud Hungarian side Ferencvaros 6-3 on aggregate to advance to the Quarter-Final of the UEFA Cup.

Keepers Korner

The boys in black and white have always relied on a man in green to keep them on track for glory. Here are some of the greatest goalies.

Jimmy Lawrence

How frustrating it must have been for United's reserve-team goalkeepers from October 1904 to May 1922, for this was the era of a Newcastle legend, appearance record-holder Jimmy Lawrence. In his 14 seasons at St James' Park, Lawrence took part in over 500 games, if you take into account the war years: that record is unlikely to be surpassed in these days of 'club hopping' and where money invariably determines a player's destiny.

It is difficult to imagine him ever having played for another club, but before moving south of the border, Lawrence turned out for Partick Athletic and Glasgow Perthshire, fitting in the odd game for Hibernian.

His timing could not have been better, for he entered a golden era during which time the First Division Championship was attained three times and the FA Cup once. Reports tell us that the Cup Finals of 1908 and 1911 were lost because of his errors, but these were obviously uncharacteristic lapses, bearing in mind the longevity of his service.

His international appearances were restricted to one in 1911 against England, a small return for such a grand servant of the game, but not a situation likely to have phased the naturally good-humoured Lawrence at a time when such fixtures carried rather less importance than today.

He stayed in the north-east after hanging up his boots, moving into League management with South Shields, progressing to Preston North End and – unusually for the time – taking a job as coach to Karlsruhe in Germany. At the time of his death in 1934 he was chairman of Stranraer.

JIMMY LAWRENCE UNITED APPS 1904-22				
League	FA Cup	League Cup	Europe	Total
432	64	—	—	496

Ronnie Simpson

Like fellow Scot Lawrence, Ronnie Simpson seemed destined to play forever – and just when most players would have been thinking of calling it a day, his finest hour arrived. Simpson already had a number of years of experience with Queens Park and Third Lanark under his belt before becoming a United player, signing for £8,750 in February 1951. The following season saw him take over from Jack Fairbrother who had suffered a broken collar-bone, making his debut in the 1-0 home defeat by Bolton Wanderers.

Not a large man by modern standards, Simpson more than made up for this in his positional awareness and sharpness of movement. In 1952 and 1955, he had reason to celebrate with two FA Cup Winners' medals, and in 1953 he won the first of two 'B' international caps against England.

In 1960, after struggling with injury for a lengthy period, he headed back to Scotland and Hibernian, possibly feeling that his playing days were coming to a premature end. But this was a new beginning, as four years later Celtic claimed his signature and took him into European football, which culminated in a European Cup winner's medal in 1967. Celtic became the first British side to win the continent's premier club trophy, beating Inter Milan 2-1. In the same year Simpson also became Scotland's oldest full international at 36.

Ronnie Simpson decided to call it a day in his fortieth year and he went into local politics. He flirted only briefly with football management at Hamilton and eventually succumbed to that traditional haven for ex-footballers, the running of a public house.

RONNIE SIMPSON UNITED APPS 1951-60				
League	FA Cup	League Cup	Europe	Total
262	33	—	—	295

WILLIE McFAUL

Willie McFaul had to show admirable patience on two separate occasions during the 20-plus years he spent at St James' Park. The first was when he had to wait until his third season of 1968-69 to take over as regular keeper from Gordon Marshall, the second as he worked through the reigns of Lee, Dinnis, McGarry, Cox and Charlton before being given his chance as first-team manager.

He left Linfield in November 1966 for Tyneside and, after his breakthrough, missed few games in seven consecutive seasons. Under six feet tall, he nonetheless proved to be a pillar of consistency in both domestic and European competition. The highlight of his career was winning the

Inter-Cities Fairs Cup in 1969 after fierce battles against Sporting Lisbon, Real Zaragoza and Glasgow Rangers. A crucial penalty save in the Semi-Final versus the Scots did as much as anything to secure a Final place.

Cruelly, he only won six international caps, having the misfortune of having to compete for a regular place with Pat Jennings, one of the world's great goalkeepers. In the majority of countries his appearance tally would surely have been considerable.

In 1975, McFaul went straight from playing into a job as trainer to the juniors, which finally paid dividends in September 1985. Jack Charlton resigned under a cloud and McFaul slipped into the top job. Initially, United showed much promise under his leadership, finishing halfway up the table in 1985-86 and even higher two years later. He eventually departed St James' Park only a couple of months into the 1988-89 season, handing over to Jim Smith who failed to save the club from relegation.

WILLIE McFAUL UNITED APPS 1966-75				
League	**FA Cup**	**League Cup**	**Europe**	**Total**
290	**23**	**18**	**24**	**355**

PAVEL SRNICEK

Continental goalkeepers were always viewed in the British game as being a luxury – agile, spectacularly flamboyant individuals who had the ability to make the easy look difficult with their exaggerated approach to shot-stopping. It was also believed that they could not deal with crosses, electing to punch rather than catch – not really an element our native game could accommodate.

This theory has now been more or less refuted with many fine keepers in domestic competition, and Pavel Srnicek has been one of the longest-serving. Kevin Keegan inherited Srnicek, as Jim Smith had signed him from Banik Ostrava in January 1991 and, while not the complete answer to United's constant search for the ultimate keeper, he has stood the test of time, still remaining on Tyneside as we entered 1998.

As mentioned elsewhere, competition for the number one position at St James' Park during Srnicek's stay has always meant periods of time where the first-team berth has been shared, most recently with Shaka Hislop and Shay Given. But the Czech is known as a good club man who accepts the situation.

Certainly the competitive aspect keeps both men on their toes, knowing the slightest of errors could mean a spell in the reserves. Srnicek is a fine shot-stopper but quite capable of the odd lapse, as when he was sent off against Tottenham. He will look back fondly at his days in the north-east, knowing he played some part in blowing away the prejudice regarding non-British goalkeepers.

PAVEL SRNICEK UNITED APPS 1991-(97)				
League	FA Cup	League Cup	Europe	Total
148	11	11	10	180

SHAKA HISLOP

Standing an impressive six foot six inches, giant keeper Shaka Hislop has battled Pavel Srnicek for a first team place since Kevin Keegan paid more than £1 million to bring him north from Reading in the summer of 1995.

Dropped to the subs' bench after the opening-day defeat at Everton last season, Shaka had to wait until the final game of 1996 to regain his Premiership place, coming back for the 7-1 demolition of Tottenham. Once back in the side, the London-born colossus maintained his position as Kenny

Dalglish succeeded Kevin Keegan in the manager's hotseat.

During Hislop's first season on Tyneside, he kept five clean sheets in his first 17 Premiership outings before being injured at Chelsea shortly before Christmas. He was restored to the side for the last seven games of the season, conceding only five goals as Newcastle ended up in second place.

That runners-up spot wasn't the only disappointment in Hislop's career. In his final game for Reading he saw Bolton Wanderers come from two down at half-time to win 4-3 at Wembley in the 1995 play-off final.

Reading had been particularly unfortunate to be in the play-offs after finishing second in a season when only the Champions were guaranteed promotion. Shaka had been an ever present in Reading's line-up, keeping 17 clean sheets and earning rave reviews for a series of brilliant performances. His role in Reading's rise was recognised with his inclusion in the PFA First Division Select XI and the Reading Player of the Year award.

It was a remarkable achievement for Reading, who had only been promoted from the Second Division a year earlier. On that occasion they'd come up as Champions, with Hislop again an ever present, conceding less than a goal a game and keeping 16 clean sheets, including five in successive matches.

Hislop was already 23 when he joined Reading in September 1992, making his debut the same month in a 3-0 defeat against West Brom at the Hawthorns. Although he had such a late start to his professional career, keepers tend to reach their peak later than outfield players, so Shaka's best years are undoubtedly still ahead.

SHAKA HISLOP UNITED APPS 1995-(97)				
League	FA Cup	League Cup	Europe	Total
40	3	5	2	50

Best Season 3

The unthinkable had almost happened in 1991-92 – relegation to Division Three, a level hitherto unknown to St James' Park.

Thanks to some gritty performances, driven on from the bench by Kevin Keegan and Terry McDermott, the drop had been avoided. Now playing in the reconstituted Division One, it was the Premiership the new management team had their eyes on.

With Sir John Hall bankrolling Keegan's ambitions to the hilt, new faces such as full-backs John Beresford and Barry Venison and midfielder Paul Bracewell were soon evident. A club record £700,000 secured Robert Lee from Charlton, while Scott Sellars and Mark Robinson were signed up in quick succession. Insurance for the future materialised in March in the shape of striker Andy Cole, even though United were by that time riding high at the top of the division.

Even in the pre-Cole days of that season, few doubted that United were Premiership-bound. From the opening game, when Southend became their first victims, to the finale against Leicester, side after side was swept away by the attacking philosophy instilled into Keegan's Magpies. Suddenly, United were the team everybody had to take notice of and the style they brought to the game had many admirers.

The first 11 League games realised as many wins, with a goal tally of 25 scored and seven conceded; a ten-point gap opened up at the top of the table, crowds had risen, and Tyneside was in carnival mood. From mid-September to the end of the season United remained on top and home games eventually became all-ticket affairs.

In a season of almost continuous success, Keegan is quoted as saying how much pleasure he received from seeing players develop, particularly individuals like Steve Howey whom he converted from a forward into an international-class defender.

When Andy Cole joined in the fun, Premiership football looked almost a certainty – 11 goals in as many games ensuring the title. That final game versus Leicester City witnessed Keegan's team in full and glorious flow, destroying the opposition by seven goals to one, both Cole and Kelly scoring hat-tricks. The points total of 96 proved to be a club record, achieved with a panache and swagger beloved by football followers the world over.

1992-93 LEAGUE RECORD

Opponents	Home	Away
Barnsley	6-0	0-1
Birmingham City	2-2	3-2
Brentford	5-1	2-1
Bristol City	5-0	2-1
Bristol Rovers	0-0	2-1
Cambridge United	4-1	3-0
Charlton Athletic	2-2	3-1
Derby County	1-1	2-1
Grimsby Town	0-1	2-0
Leicester City	7-1	1-2
Luton Town	2-0	0-0
Millwall	1-1	2-1
Notts County	4-0	2-0
Oxford United	2-1	2-4
Peterborough United	3-0	1-0
Portsmouth	3-1	0-2
Southend United	3-2	1-1
Sunderland	1-0	2-1
Swindon Town	0-0	1-2
Tranmere Rovers	1-0	3-0
Watford	2-0	0-1
West Ham United	2-0	0-0
Wolverhampton Wanderers	2-1	0-1

Through The Years
November

1905
November
11

United equalled their record victory by demolishing Wolves 8-0. Bill Appleyard netted a hat-trick and Ronald Orr chipped in with two. Three years later another eight-goal haul saw the Magpies celebrate as Birmingham were dismissed.

1942
November
14

Playing as a guest, Tom Finney scored a hat-trick against Gateshead in a Football League, Northern Section game. In November 1944, again in the Northern Section, United won successive games 7-0, 6-3 and 11-0, Edward Carr (guesting from Arsenal) scoring nine goals in the three games.

1950
November
25

The Magpies beat Charlton 3-2, having been two goals down with ten minutes to go. The points were secured thanks to goals from Jackie Milburn (two) and Tommy Walker.

1959
November
27

Nothing could have prepared United for today's events. Coming into the home game against Everton they had lost three games on the trot but hit devastating form to win 8-2, Len White (three) and Ivor Allchurch (two) among the scorers. Charlie Mitten's side suddenly looked less like relegation candidates.

1962
November

Bryan 'Pop' Robson, a striker destined to become one of United's most popular players, was signed from local club Clara Vale. He had to wait nearly two years to make his first-team debut, but would prove an invaluable asset.

1993
November
21

Andy Cole scored a hat-trick inside 30 minutes in a 3-0 victory over Liverpool, indicating that United, still regarded in some quarters as Premiership new boys, were determined to make a serious Championship challenge.

GREAT DEFENDERS

Though they're traditionally known as an attack-minded club, Newcastle United have nurtured some stylish stoppers over the years.

FRANK BRENNAN

Frank Brennan became something of a Tyneside idol just after World War II, retaining the fans' affections until his departure in 1956. A big man in every sense, Brennan epitomised the commanding centre-half around whom so many managers of the era would build their defence.

Stan Seymour signed him from Airdrie in May 1946, putting into place one of the components which would lead to promotion within two seasons, his debut against Millwall, in August 1946 heralding a special era for United. During the 1947-48 season he was an ever-present, as the Magpies finished in second position and Milburn and company found themselves back in Division One, Brennan's towering presence a major contributory factor.

The top division was where Frank Brennan deserved to perform, and representative honours came his way as he established himself as one of the best centre-halves in the home countries. Many would argue that he deserved far more than his seven Scotland caps.

He became an FA Cup winner in successive seasons, but

missed out on the 1955 victory over Manchester City as first-team outings became less frequent. In keeping with so many other United players over the years he fell out with the directors, the ensuing dispute being a forerunner of the much-publicised Eastham affair.

The situation was clearly intolerable and in 1956 he left for North Shields, a sad ending for a folk hero. He continued with that club in later years as both a coach and manager, and much pleasure must have come his way in 1969 when he guided North Shields to FA Amateur Cup Final success at Wembley, scene of his greatest triumphs.

FRANK BRENNAN UNITED RECORD 1946-56

League		FA Cup		League Cup		Europe		Total	
Apps	Goals	Apps	Goals	Apps	Goals	Apps	Goals	Apps	Goals
318	3	29	—	—	—	—	—	347	3

FRANK CLARK

When asking any Geordie fan for their list of all-time favourite players, you could put your money on Frank Clark's name being in there with the greatest names. For season after season nobody expected the Number 3 shirt to be filled by anyone else. Clark was a dependable rather than inspired practitioner, adhering to the basics which he performed rather well and rejecting the more flamboyant aspects of the game. Arguably, he represented the perfect full-back.

Signing from Crook Town in 1962, he had to wait some time before making his first appearance, towards the close of the 1963-64 season. From then on he became a regular, and won a medal in his first full season as the Second Division Championship came to St James' Park.

He only experienced First Division football after that, sharing also in the elation of winning the Inter-Cities Fairs Cup and the humiliation of FA Cup Final defeat. His consistent performances also won him a place in the Football League side which competed against the League of Ireland in 1970, his only representative honour.

In a surprise move in 1975, the astute Brian Clough whisked Clark away on a free transfer to Nottingham Forest, much to the chagrin of Geordie supporters. This presented him with a further European challenge, resulting in a second lease of life and a European Cup winner's medal.

Upon retirement he became assistant manager at Sunderland, coached at Forest and became managing director at Leyton Orient after a spell as manager. He eventually took over the Brian Clough role at Forest, struggling to bring back the glory days without success, and later moved on to Manchester City.

FRANK CLARK UNITED RECORD 1962-75

League		FA Cup		League Cup		Europe		Total	
Apps	Goals	Apps	Goals	Apps	Goals	Apps	Goals	Apps	Goals
389	—	26	—	19	1	23	—	457	1

Bobby Moncur

In many respects, craggy Scot Moncur carried on the Frank Brennan tradition with his powerful displays at the centre of the defence, although he could fill the position of sweeper as well as the functions of the old-fashioned centre-half. Despite possessing all the credentials of an aggressive defender, Moncur had a cultured edge which singled him out as a very special player. Joining United in 1960, he became part of United's fine youth team which tasted success in the Final of the FA Youth Cup in 1962, but had to be patient before establishing himself as a first-team regular.

Clearly Joe Harvey did not want to rush the inexperienced Moncur and it was not until the 1965-66 season that he became a familiar face in the black and white stripes. Two years later he was captaining the side and looking to add a full international cap to the Under-23 honour he had already received. He did not have long to wait, winning his first cap in 1968 and being made Scotland's captain after only a handful of games.

Like Frank Clark, he experienced the ups and downs of Cup football; in the Inter-Cities Fairs Cup, where he fulfilled the hero's role and the 1974 FA Cup Final, after which his services were deemed no longer required. Moving to Sunderland, he shared in the Wearsiders promotion season of 1975-76, retiring thereafter to pursue a mixture of sporting interests.

Carlisle, Hearts, Plymouth Argyle and Hartlepool employed him as manager but yachting, his other great passion, took up a high percentage of his time and in 1985 he participated in the gruelling Around Britain Race. No doubt he took to the water the same highly professional skills he carried onto the football pitch.

BOBBY MONCUR UNITED RECORD 1960-76

League		FA Cup		League Cup		Europe		Total	
Apps	Goals	Apps	Goals	Apps	Goals	Apps	Goals	Apps	Goals
296	3	18	1	10	—	22	4	346	8

Darren Peacock

In his search for a commanding central defender, Kevin Keegan settled on Queens Park Ranger Darren Peacock as the man to bolster his sometimes susceptible defence. Just beating the transfer deadline in March 1994, Peacock took a while to find his feet in a defence unsettled by injuries. Once he had established himself, Peacock became the rock his manager knew he would be.

Darren made his United debut in a comfortable 3-0 home win over Norwich after signing for £2,700,000, and has been a regular in the side ever since. He'd made his League debut while still an apprentice with former League club Newport County.

He had come a long way from his birthplace of Bristol and those initial games for Newport. His next port of call had been Hereford United, for whom he played nearly 60 League games before becoming part of the Rangers set-up.

At the start of the 1994-95 season, Philippe Albert was introduced into the side and proved to be a perfect foil for Peacock. The Belgian's liking for forays into the opposition half sometimes left space behind him, but gave his partner the chance to show what an accomplished, combative player he had become. In a side bristling with talent, Peacock has never been found wanting.

The pony-tailed defender was many people's choice as 1996-97's Player of the Year, winning over his critics through his consistently excellent performances. A commanding player, Peacock reads the game well and is quick to attack the ball.

As a regular in the side which finished in runners-up spot in two successive seasons, Peacock must have wondered whether his best chance of a League winners' medal had disappeared as 1997-98 rolled on and the Magpies were clearly not going to trouble the front-runners. Rumours abounded regarding a clearout of players, Peacock's name among them – but whether staying in the north-east or moving elsewhere, he will guarantee total commitment. There are still plenty of games left in those 30-year-old legs.

DARREN PEACOCK UNITED RECORD 1994-(97)									
League		FA Cup		League Cup		Europe		Total	
Apps	Goals	Apps	Goals	Apps	Goals	Apps	Goals	Apps	Goals
113	2	10	—	10	2	12	—	145	4

The War Years

While wartime football may have come as a welcome break from the austerity and despair that conflicts bring, the make-up of the various competitions and the footballing standards on offer were largely unrecognisable.

In the First World War, the Magpies were reluctant to participate in anything approaching organised football, and friendlies became the order of the day. It was not until 1917-18 that United felt it necessary to enter a team in the Newcastle and District League, very much a secondary competition made up of lesser local sides. United were nowhere near full strength and only fleetingly would a well-known name be seen sporting the black and white stripes.

In 1919 the Northern Victory League was formed to celebrate the end of hostilities and more familiar faces could be seen back in United colours. The Magpies could finish only fifth in a league of eight teams, winning just five games out of 14. The competition ran from 11 January to the end of April, St James' crowds averaging an encouraging 22,000: the home attendance for the South Shields game was 40,000.

In 1939 the season was only three games old when the League shut-down occurred, just after what turned out to be a meaningless 8-1 victory over Swansea. Most of the players who commenced that season managed to see out the alternative competitions introduced, United taking part in the North East Regional League and League War Cup. Second place was achieved in the former and a Semi-Final place in the latter. For their final two League games Newcastle fielded two entirely different teams on the same day, beating Leeds and losing to Bradford.

The football authorities decided to regionalise the League Championship and 1941-42 found United competing in the Northern section which split into separate championships. One ran from August to December, the other taking place from March to May, while sandwiched in-between came the Football League North Cup. It must have all seemed very strange to those used to the normal Football League season.

So football continued with its strange structure until the advent of the 1945-46 campaign when, in anticipation of a return to normality, a full 42-game programme was re-introduced. The League was split into Northern and Southern sections and the FA Cup reinstated.

The war years had seen Albert Stubbins running amok in opposition defences. His achievements have been underplayed due to the generally poor quality of wartime football – but all his 232 goals scored during the period had to be worked for. Four successive seasons of 40 goals or more remain an impressive testament to Stubbins' finishing powers, and it was no surprise that he went on to greater things with Liverpool.

The legendary name of Jackie Milburn first appeared on the team sheet in 1943-44 when he played in 24 games and scored 12 goals. In all, 'Wor Jackie' made 95 wartime appearances, claiming 38 goals at the start of his most distinguished career.

The introduction of guest players had a novelty value but did nothing for team continuity, and Newcastle's only trophy was the Tyne-Tees Cup won in 1944. Famous names to don the black and white stripes included Bill Nicholson (Tottenham), Jimmy Mullen (Wolves) and Tom Finney (Preston). Stan Mortensen played one game in 1943, claiming two goals in a 9-0 hammering of Leeds, with Stubbins grabbing three and Mullen chipping in with two of his own.

Gafferspeak

Managers of Newcastle United are used to being the talk of the Toon. Here's some talk of their own.

'I have longed for the day when the place was buzzing with people. Now that day has arrived.'

Arthur Cox in 1982 after signing Kevin Keegan.

'How he never won an England cap never ceases to amaze me'

Joe Harvey on consistent and loyal full-back Bobby Cowell.

'There will be no stars on Tyneside.'

Gordon Lee outlines his philosophy on joining the club.

'We never got started, and I'll never understand it to this day.'

Joe Harvey on the 1974 Wembley defeat

'Sometimes he would make me tear my hair out.'

Kevin Keegan describes moulding Robert Lee into the perfect midfielder.

'No one player is more important than the club.'

Kenny Dalglish on Faustino Asprilla, shortly before his multi-million pound transfer back to Parma.

'David Craig's was the first name I put on my team sheet.'

Joe Harvey paying the ultimate compliment to a full-back selected on over 400 occasions.

'I've never played in nor seen a Cup Final to match this game for fighting courage.'

An elated Joe Harvey on his team after the second leg of the Inter-Cities Fairs Cup Final in 1969.

'Scoring means a lot to him. He is desperate to succeed at the highest level.'

Kenny Dalglish trying to explain Temuri Ketsbaia's extraordinary celebrations after scoring against Bolton Wanderers in January 1998.

'No other player in the world could have had such a dramatic effect on the club and its supporters.'

Arthur Cox in 1984 on Kevin Keegan.

'If Kevin Keegan fell in the Tyne, he'd come up with a salmon in his mouth.' *Jack Charlton*

'Terry had a left foot like a wand.'

Joe Harvey waxing lyrical on Terry Hibbitt.

'If anybody was wondering why they call him Supermac, then they will be in no doubt now.'

Joe Harvey, this time on Malcolm Macdonald.

'Kevin phoned and said, We're going back, pal! We're going to change that club round.'

Terry McDermott recalls Keegan's clarion call

'We used to say Tommy Walker could catch pigeons, he was so quick.'

Ex-United stalwart and Sunderland manager Bob Stokoe on his ex-colleague.

Through The Years
December

1892
December
24

Formed out of the East End club, Newcastle United FC played its first ever match in a friendly against Middlesbrough.

1907
December
26

When Bill Appleyard scored against Sheffield United on Boxing Day, he completed a sequence of having scored in eight out of the last nine games.

1925
December
12

One of United's most treasured acquisitions Hughie Gallagher moved south of the border from Airdrie to start his love affair with the St James' Park faithful. He scored twice today on his debut in a 3-3 draw with Everton.

1955

December

Although a month of fluctuating fortunes for the club, marksmen Vic Keeble and Jackie Milburn were in their element. Twenty goals were scored in seven games, with Keeble claiming eight of them and Milburn seven. The month included two most satisfying successive results, when local rivals Sunderland were defeated twice, with a goal tally of 9-2.

1964

December

In a season which ended in a triumphant return to Division One, this turned out to be one of the best months in the club's history. Five games were played and won, 13 goals scored and one in reply, with a double completed over Middlesbrough.

1996

December

28

Having gone seven League games without a win, the Magpies turned this post-Christmas game against Tottenham into a rout; Shearer, Ferdinand and Lee all scored twice in a 7-1 seasonal gift for Geordie fans.

The Kitbag

The black and white stripes associated with Newcastle United that gave them their 'Magpies' nickname may not have changed, but the presentation of the club badge, collar style and kitmaker's name has varied widely over the seasons.

The sponsors of Newcastle United have remained constant since the concept was introduced in the mid 1980s. Scottish and Newcastle Breweries, have kept their badge on the chests of the Magpies, initially just as a blue star. They then pushed the McEwan's Lager brand – currently the name seen on the chest of Glasgow Rangers – and eventually Greenalls (at the same time as the badge turned from a crest into a horrible psychedelic 'NUFC'), but these days the logo is the yellow and white label-shape oval that identifies their most famous product, the legendary Newcastle Brown Ale.

Between the wars, Newcastle players wore a round-neck shirt with a drawstring which, by the time of Jackie Milburn and the Cup kings of the 1950s, had become a rugby-style garment. The era of Gascoigne, Keegan and Waddle was one in which a black stripe was at the centre of the shirt (as opposed to white now), with a black collar. The club badge was neatly encased in a circular border with the maker's badge (Umbro) in a similarly prominent position on the right.

The mid 1990s, at the time of Alan Shearer's arrival, saw a rugby-style collar return to the shirt with black and white stripes very much wider than previously. The club badge and Adidas logo were on left and right of the sponsor's logo, the central focal point of the shirt – as is so often the case these days.

Black shorts are normal wear: the current design has an embroidered club badge on the right leg and Adidas on the left leg. The socks – currently black, though white was worn in the 1970s – have three white stripes, identified with the Adidas brand, with a white band round the sock with a badge, NUFC above and Adidas below.

The goalkeeper's shirt, multicoloured earlier in the decade, is now a bright emerald green (adopted in homage to Eire international Shay Given, perhaps?) and has an almost imitation crocodile-skin texture to it, black collar with Adidas logo and cuffs. Shorts are long and baggy, old-style, with the ubiquitous blue star ar either side and a drawstring at the front.

Away kits have changed frequently over the years. The 1980s, when Kevin Keegan was a player, saw a classy grey/silver, while the mid 1990s saw an attractive mix of maroon and blue hoops with white shorts, multicoloured socks and a white button collar. The current kit, introduced in 1997, is dark blue with orange stripes from neck to arm, plus a green and orange stripe down the right hand side of the shirt. The sponsor's badge, a simpler 'Newcastle Brown' design, is placed on this stripe, with a club crest on a shield shape counterbalancing on the left breast.

There has, however, been at least one problem, when a referee had to don a borrowed sweatshirt because he found Newcastle United players passing to him! No danger of that with the away goalkeeper's kit – a bright orange with black concentric circles radiating away from the sponsor's outsize logo placed low on the right side. Even the official merchandise catalogue described this as 'a real eye-opener'! It's unfortunate, though, that it's sponsor's logo that is the focus of the kit and not the club crest, which is relatively inconspicuous.

It is sometimes said that player numbers are hard to see on striped shirts. Newcastle's current answer to this has been to place white numbers on a black shield shape. And just in case the stranded opposition full-back has any doubts as to who he's playing against as Keith Gillespie goes waltzing by, his shirt (not to mention his team-mates') has 'Newcastle United' emblazoned across the flapping tail.

You can order everything from bathrobes to mountain bikes from the Newcastle megastore at St James' Park – and if you can't get there in person, you can visit the store on the Internet if you aim to be kitted out in style.

EUROPEAN CUP

The Magpies qualified through the back door first time out – but you can bet it won't be the last!

Stage	Opponents	Home	Away	Agg
1997-98				
Qualifier 1	NK Croatia Zagreb	2-1	2-2	4-3
Group C	Barcelona	3-2	—	—
Group C	Dinamo Kiev	—	2-2	—
Group C	PSV Eindhoven	—	0-1	—
Group C	PSV Eindhoven	0-2	—	—
Group C	Barcelona	—	0-1	—
Group C	Dinamo Kiev	2-0	—	—

Newcastle failed to qualify for Quarter-Final

Inter-Cities Fairs/UEFA Cup

The first European campaign was attended by success as Newcastle brought back the Fairs Cup.

Stage	Opponents	Home	Away	Agg
1968-69				
Round 1	Feyenoord	4-0	0-2	4-2
Round 2	Sporting Lisbon	1-0	1-1	2-1
Round 3	Real Zaragoza	2-1	2-3	4-4
	Newcastle won on away goals			
Quarter-Final	Vitoria Setubal	5-1	1-3	6-4
Semi-Final	Rangers	2-0	0-0	2-0
Final	Ujpest Dozsa	3-0	3-2	6-2
1969-70				
Round 1	Dundee United	1-0	2-1	3-1
Round 2	Porto	1-0	0-0	1-0
Round 3	Southampton	0-0	1-1	1-1
	Newcastle won on away goals			
Quarter-Final	Anderlecht	3-1	0-2	3-3
	Newcastle lost on away goals			

Stage	Opponents	Home	Away	Agg
1970-71				
Round 1	Inter Milan	2-0	1-1	3-1
Round 2	Pecsi Dozsa	2-0	0-2	2-2
	Newcastle lost on penalties			
1977-78				
Round 1	Bohemians	4-0	0-0	4-0
Round 2	Bastia	1-3	1-2	2-5
1994-95				
Round 1	Antwerp	5-2	5-0	10-2
Round 2	Atletico Bilbao	3-2	0-1	3-3
	Newcastle lost on away goals			
1996-97				
Round 1	Halmstad	4-0	1-2	5-2
Round 2	Ferencvaros	4-0	2-3	6-3
Round 3	Metz	2-0	1-1	3-1
Quarter-Final	Monaco	0-1	0-3	0-4

Newcastle's record against European opposition

Country	P	W	D	L	F-A
Belgium	4	3	—	1	13-5
Croatia	2	1	1	—	4-3
Eire	2	1	1	—	4-0
England	2	—	2	—	1-1
France	6	1	1	4	5-10
Holland	4	1	—	3	4-5
Hungary	6	4	—	2	14-7
Italy	2	1	1	—	3-1
Portugal	6	3	2	1	9-5
Scotland	4	3	1	—	5-1
Spain	6	3	—	3	10-10
Sweden	2	1	—	1	5-2
Ukraine	2	1	1	—	4-2

Substitutes

With the number of substitutes clubs can have on the bench at any one game having been increased to three in the League and five in the FA Cup, their tactical use will clearly have a bearing on each and every game.

Newcastle records show the number of substitutes making a major contribution to a game is minimal. The one major exception involves forward Alan Foggon, who came off the bench to hit the winner in the second leg of the Inter-Cities Fairs Cup Final against Ujpest Dozsa in 1969, thereby ensuring the winning of United's first European trophy. On the domestic front, Scots striker Alex Mathie (now with Ipswich) came on to blast Newcastle's Goal of the Season against Sheffield Wednesday in September 1993.

We've come a long way since Albert Bennett sat out the game as United's first official substitute on 21 August 1965 in a game versus Nottingham Forest, and Ollie Burton had the honour of being the first substitute to be used two weeks later. In fact it was Burton who became the first United player to come off the bench and score in a League Cup tie against Lincoln City on 13 September 1967.

To prove how far the mighty can fall, Mirandinha found himself on the bench on seven occasions in 1988-89, his sidelining in only his second season at St James' Park proving the Brazilian's honeymoon was over under new boss Jim Smith. Adding insult to injury, he was substituted in half of his 22 League starts. During the same season John Robertson made it on to the field in seven consecutive games, having been awarded the number 12 shirt for each fixture, while Gary Brazil started a total of 23 games on the bench in 1989-90 but only got on in 12: coincidentally, his Newcastle career only ran to 23 League appearances.

Yet when Alan Shearer came back from serious injury in January 1998, he seemed intent on writing himself yet again into the club history books. His header back across goal was instrumental in setting up Ketsbaia's winning goal against Bolton at the Reebok Stadium. The Magpies' record buy had been on the pitch just 18 minutes, and not only set up the Georgian's goal but retrieved his shirt from the crowd after the extrovert midfielder had thrown it to the fans. If any substitute was going to swing the game, his actions suggested, you'd have put your shirt on Shearer…

DREAM TEAM 3

Some might not agree that 1996-97 proved to be the best of seasons for United – but for one brief, shining moment, as in 1926-27, the Geordies were privileged to witness some dazzling football.

Goalkeeper **Shaka Hislop**
The giant ex-Reading keeper had to fight for a regular place, as he and Pavel Srnicek competed for the Number 1 shirt.

Right-back **Warren Barton**
Only forced himself into a regular spot in February but proved to be an excellent club man.

Left-back **Robbie Elliott**
Mysteriously transferred to Bolton in the summer, some believe his full potential has yet to be realised.

Central defender **Darren Peacock**
Performed to a consistently high standard since being acquired from Queens Park Rangers, making the Number 5 shirt his own.

Central defender **Philippe Albert**

Albert is a sight to behold in full flow, his cavalier attitude to defensive duties making him popular on the terraces if not in the dugout.

Midfielder **David Batty**

Even more valuable on Tyneside than at Elland Road, his contribution in the middle of the park is crucial to United's well-being.

Midfielder **John Beresford**

One of the longest-serving players on the current Magpies staff, the left-sided Beresford arrived via Portsmouth and had played over 160 games prior to the 1997-98 season.

Midfielder **Lee Clark**

Played in nearly 200 games before moving to Sunderland. Highly talented individual on the fringes of England recognition who found lack of consistency his main problem.

Midfield **Robert Lee**

At the close of the 1996–97 season Lee had added 181 League games to nearly 300 for Charlton Athletic. It is difficult to imagine the present side functioning without him.

Forward **Les Ferdinand**

Despite his 17 League and Cup goals, Londoner Ferdinand returned to the capital with Tottenham at a time when the fans expected his partnership with Alan Shearer to bear fruit.

Forward **Alan Shearer**

Shearer had an excellent start to his Newcastle career, providing evidence of true world class and promising much for forthcoming seasons – injury permitting.

Worst Season 3

If ever a side looked like relegation candidates from day one of a season, it was the Magpies, who lost their opening fixture to Everton 4-0 on 27 August 1988.

Losing three out of their four opening games meant United faced an uphill struggle which they never looked like coming to grips with, even though the away win at Liverpool in October generated false optimism for some diehard supporters. Although three 4-0 defeats were the most humiliating moments of the League campaign, going out of both Cup competitions to opposition from lower divisions was a pointer to where United were heading.

A best League position of 17th which only stood for one game (the second) indicated tough times ahead for a side that simply could not score goals. Only 30 League goals in the season, nine of those from a far from convincing Mirandinha, brightened the months of pain for the watching St James' Park fans.

By Christmas, manager Willie McFaul had been replaced by Jim Smith who would continue to fight a losing battle, a major problem Smith also had to face involved Mirandinha, with whom he had no empathy. The clash of personalities did nothing to further United's cause and, as the Brazilian had only netted three times up to the new year, the club's great hope was clearly not the answer to Tyneside's prayers.

As already indicated, it was lack of goals that sealed United's fate; the combative David McCreery and steadfast Glenn Roeder, members of a previously successful United side, were simply not able to hold together a team with too many anonymous faces. Thirty-five players were used in the fruitless search for a line-up to save the sinking ship.

Only seven League wins and 21 losses are statistics which spell problems for any club, particularly when the season included a nine-game period where United only scored in one game – even if it was a 3-0 triumph over local rivals Middlesbrough. The final run-in of nine games without a win booked the relegation ticket.

The close season saw the departure of the admirable McCreery to Hearts and the first steps taken to hasten the return to Brazil of Mirandinha, the club's most expensive misfit. Jim Smith had to take a step downwards to carry the club into the upwardly mobile 1990s.

1988-89 LEAGUE RECORD

Opponents	Home	Away
Arsenal	0-1	0-1
Aston Villa	1-2	1-3
Charlton Athletic	0-2	2-2
Coventry City	0-3	2-1
Derby County	0-1	0-2
Everton	2-0	0-4
Liverpool	2-2	2-1
Luton Town	0-0	0-0
Manchester United	0-0	0-2
Middlesbrough	3-0	1-1
Millwall	1-1	0-4
Norwich City	0-2	2-0
Nottingham Forest	0-1	1-1
Queens Park Rangers	1-2	0-3
Sheffield Wednesday	1-3	2-1
Southampton	3-3	0-1
Tottenham Hotspur	2-2	0-2
West Ham United	1-2	0-2
Wimbledon	2-1	0-4

United's All-Time Roll Of Honour

1897-98	Division Two Runners-up
1904-05	Division One Champions and FA Cup Runners-up
1905-06	FA Cup Runners-up
1906-07	Division One Champions
1907-08	FA Cup Runners-up
1908-09	Division One Champions
1909-10	FA Cup Winners
1910-11	FA Cup Runners-up
1923-24	FA Cup Winners
1926-27	Division One Champions
1931-32	FA Cup Winners
1947-48	Division Two Runners-up
1950-51	FA Cup Winners
1951-52	FA Cup Winners
1954-55	FA Cup Winners
1964-65	Division Two Champions
1968-69	Inter-Cities Fairs Cup Winners
1972-73	Anglo-Italian Cup Winners
1973-74	FA Cup Runners-up and Texaco Cup Winners

1974-75	Texaco Cup Winners
1975-76	League Cup Runners-up
1992-93	Division One (old Two) Champions
1995-96	Premier League Runners-up
1996-97	Premier League Runners-up

Quiz Answers

See page 120-123 for questions.

1 Willie McFaul

2 Parma

3 Carlisle United

4 Queens Park Rangers

5 David Ginola

6 Nottingham Forest

7 Tottenham Hotspur

8 The Anglo-Italian Cup

9 The Bear

10 Arsenal

11 Sunderland

12 Fulham and Luton

13 Manchester City

14 Third

15 Bob Stokoe

16 Airdrie

17 Jackie Milburn

18 George Robledo

19 Ards

20 Manchester City

21 Mike Channon

22 Pat Howard

23 Jimmy Scoular

24 Liverpool

25 Sheffield Wednesday

26 Ronnie Simpson

27 One

28 David McCreery

29 Pearson

30 Hughie Gallagher

31 Denmark

32 112

33 1992

34 Four

35 Jimmy Smith

36 Mick Quinn

37 Richard Dinnis

38 RSC Anderlecht

39 Linfield

40 Ruel Fox

THE LAST WORD

'Newcastle is light years away from what the club was when Gazza was here - the club is probably too big for him now.'

Sir John Hall, 1995